THE PATH OF SHE
BOOK OF SABBATS

Karen Clark

SheBard Media Inc.

Clark, Karen 1961-

ISBN 978-0-9936919-2-8

Cover design by SheBard Media Inc. Cover photo: Barclay
Sound, Vancouver Island, British Columbia. Interior photos:
Salt Spring Island, British Columbia.

For Nature and the Mysteries: our great teachers and guides in the turning of the seasons on our journey of soul, and for the powerful, beautiful kindred spirits who have woven Sabbat magic with me and enriched my spiritual dance with the seasons.

CONTENTS

A Journey of Soul

Your journey of soul
leads you home
to the living ways
of Nature, without,
and your Deep Self, within.
Where you seek one,
you will find the other.

Take a moment to step outside your door. See the sky, smell the air, feel the press of humidity and temperature on your flesh, heed the quality of the light and colors of the landscape, and notice what the plants and animals are up to. Open to the kiss of sunshine on your skin, or the wetness of rain, or the nip of frost, or the bite of the wind, or however else you experience the season and weather of the day.

Breathe deep and settle into your creature instincts, the part of you that knows that your engagement of Nature matters to you, deeply.

This is your home, without, this Earth. Your human form has emerged from and evolved out of the material elements that constitute all things of this living world. Physically and energetically you are inextricably linked to Nature's seasons and conditions. Whether you live in close communion with the wild realm or in a crowded city, still it is the mingling of sun, soil, rain and seed, and the natural resources of this planet that feed, clothe and house you, and on which our continued human existence depends.

Witness the trees reaching their limbs toward the sun, the birds' effortless navigation of the air space, and the myriad of ways that the wild things around you are seamlessly expressing their innate essence through their form and actions. There is a place and purpose for all living things of this world, each in accordance with the unique, luminescent spark of Creation at its core.

Breathe deep and settle into your Deep Self, the part of you that holds your spark of Creation, and place and purpose in the great weaving of life.

This too is your home, within. Here you find your true

beauty and gifts, and your innate, indisputable worthiness and authenticity. Like the wild things you are witnessing, you were put on this Earth to live and flourish from your Deep Self outward. And in the most secret places inside of you, your soul longs for your outer life to be a seamless expression of this inner wellspring of beauty and potential.

Our home on this Earth and our home within our Deep Self are entwined reflections of our authentic humanity. We are magnificent beings, woven of light and matter, an immortal soul encased in the mortal coil of flesh and bones.

Like all living things of our Earth home, our life is governed by the turnings of the Cosmos and the laws of physical existence. The dance of these elemental forces reveals itself in the cycle of Nature, and of our life story, through the seasons of light and dark, life and death, and joy and sorrow. And just like our wild kin, our life story is sourced from the inner spark of Creation of our Deep Self.

In our modern society, with its homocentric attitude toward Nature and disconnect from the inner stirrings of soul, we have abandoned our roots in these primal, vital manifestations of home, within and without.

We can go about our everyday existence paying little attention to what is happening outside our door in the natural realm. Through the turn of a thermostat, flick of a light switch or trip to the local grocery store with its worldwide access to foodstuff, we seem to transcend Nature's travels through the seasons of light, life, darkness and death that ordered and suffused the lives of our pagan, agrarian ancestors.

This same disregard extends to our inner, spiritual landscape. We collectively suffer from a myopic fixation on things of mind and materiality, and order our sense of self and external life in accordance with outer-imposed norms and ideals.

While our soul longs for an authentic existence, living from the inside-out of our Deep Self, social conditioning entrains us to homogeneity and conformity rather than the discovery and expression of our individual beauty and gifts.

In this profound disconnect from Nature and our Deep Self, we have lost our way, forgetting who we are, what we are made of, and how to best navigate and flourish in this tricky business of life. And from this disconnect, a vast, voracious hunger arises that expresses itself in the dysfunction and malaise that haunt our personal life and shared society. So much of the harm we do to ourselves, each other and this wondrous Earth springs from the simple, overshadowing fact that we do not live in loving, respectful communion with our Deep Self and Nature.

It is this very hunger that sets us on our journey of soul. Though we may have many positives in our life, deep, deep inside, we sense that something essential is missing. We long for more meaning, more presence, more connection, more joy, more contentment, and below this, we hunger for more of powerful forces that we can sense but not name. We know, in our sweet hopes and best instincts, that a richer, fuller life is possible, as is a human society based on generosity, goodness and a sustainable relationship with the Earth.

Breathe deep and say hello to your own sacred hunger, the part of you that understands and responds to these words.

Your journey of soul beckons, calling you to step past the life and world that you know in search of home within and without, and your true, most beautiful Self.

Your Journey of Soul Across the Seasons

There are many spiritual paths and ways to frame and engage our journey of soul in search of meaning, purpose and home within the immense mysteries and powers of life. A pagan perspective honors the primacy of Nature and our inner Divinity, our home without and within, in our spiritual pathwork of healing and transformation.

Nature is our great ally on our journey of soul. What we have forgotten, Nature remembers. Each season seamlessly expresses different aspects of the elemental forces that shape life on Earth, written large in the sensual language of what we can see, feel, hear, smell and taste of Nature's physical displays and offerings. And within these physical displays and energetic forces, we can discover the profound teachings and mysteries that illuminate our human experience and life story, and guide our way home to Nature and our Deep Self.

Many pagan traditions honor the seasonal teachings and mysteries of Nature through the Wheel of the Year, with its powerful framework for engaging the energies and turnings of the seasons.

The Wheel of the Year is an annual cycle of eight Sabbats or celebration days rooted in historical pagan beliefs, traditions and practices. The year is divided into the four quarters of the Fall, Winter, Spring and Summer seasons, with four solar Sabbats falling on the Fall and Spring Equinoxes and the Winter and Summer Solstices. The other four Sabbats, known as cross-quarter days — Samhain, Imbolc, Beltane and Lammas — fall on the approximate midway points between the solar Sabbats.

These Sabbats mark potent astronomical and energetic annual events that anchor our spiritual pathwork in the outer seasonal manifestations of Nature, their mirror inner teachings, and the mysteries of the Gods and Goddesses ascribed to the celebration days.

Sabbats dates are for the Northern Hemisphere, and can vary based on the timing of Equinox and Solstice astronomical events. These dates are advanced by six months in the Southern Hemisphere to coincide with its seasons.

Just as there are many spiritual paths to guide our journey of soul, there are also various pagan traditions and practices for celebrating the Wheel of the Year. On the Path of She, the ways of the sacred feminine are integral to our journey and pathwork across the Sabbats and seasons.

The sacred feminine, in basic terms, is the feminine face of the Divine: the Goddess, the life-centered ethos of the Cosmos, and the sacred matter of the living Earth and our human body.

As the Great Goddess, She is the wellspring of life, and the shining love that infuses Creation. As the Dark Goddess, She is also death and the struggle that comes from being born of flesh and beholden to the dictates of the physical Universe. It is Her natural laws and mysteries that govern Nature's and humanity's cycles through the seasons of light and dark, life and death, and joy and sorrow.

The sacred feminine is foreign to our modern sensibilities; She has been repressed, denigrated and relegated to the fringe of our human society and psyche. And in this disregard for Her presence and powers, we have cut ourselves off from matter, Mother, Goddess, Earth, our physical body and primal home in Nature, and from Her mysteries of the sacred dark that hold the missing pieces of our authentic, whole/holy humanity, and the lost parts of our Deep Self and life story.

At this pivotal, tumultuous time in our history — a Great Turning in our human spiritual evolution — the sacred feminine is awakening in our collective and individual consciousness to guide us in the essential work of healing and transforming our lives and our world. She calls us to heed our sacred hungers, remember Her life-centered ways and our home in Nature, and reclaim the beauty and power of our Deep Self and authentic humanity.

In this call, the sacred feminine invites you to set your feet on an ancient pathway that arises from the primal powers and mysteries that govern all living things of this Earth — a path that is ever present in the cycle and seasons of Nature, and in the wisdom of the Gods and Goddesses that have guided humanity through the ages.

On the Path of She, the Wheel of the Year and this ancient pathway are merged, facilitating your journey of soul across the eight Sabbats and their seasons of darkness, death, light and life, in tandem with the ways of the sacred feminine.

The Goddess tales of Persephone and Inanna illuminate this ancient, sacred feminine pathway, offering powerful directives for your journey of soul across the seasons. In these tales, the Goddess descends into the Underworld of darkness and death, embracing its mysteries, trials and lessons, and then returns from Her journey to the sunlit realm of light and life, transformed and ready to blossom into Her full beauty and powers.

So too your journey of soul will lead you first into the seasons and mysteries of darkness, death and endings that promise new beginnings; this is the sacred dark, beyond the world that you know, with offerings that reveal the innermost roots of your healing and transformation. Know that the dark places inside of you, like life, will bring trials and lessons, and it is these very things that are the crucible of your deepest becoming.

Yet this is not a journey of despair, but one of love, hope and trust in yourself and the powers of life to lead you home as you emerge into the seasons of light, life and the blossoming outward of your true, beautiful Deep Self and authentic humanity. And this home is not some rarified, perfected state, but a complex weaving of all that you are and all that you've experienced — the light and shadow, beauty and wounding, joy and sorrow, and of things known and mysteries yet to be discovered.

Like a Goddess, you travel this ancient pathway by your own conscious choice, courage and determination. No one can make this passage for you, and no two journeys are alike. No matter whether you are new to these spiritual teachings or an experienced practitioner, you find your way home on your own terms and in your own time, in accordance with your Deep Self's essence and purpose, and the imperatives of your life story.

Though this is a solitary pathway, what heals and transforms your life, can heal and transform the world. Persephone emerges from Her Underworld travels as the Goddess of spring growth, and where She treads, She leaves a trail of flowers in Her wake. So too, in the blossoming and shining forth of your deepest beauty and gifts, you can leave a trail of new, positive possibilities in your wake that can change others and renew our world.

Nature calls you home; the sacred feminine calls you home; your Deep Self calls you home — where you seek one, you will find the others. So step onto this ancient pathway; let the Sabbats and seasons be your pave stones, and Nature and the Gods and Goddesses be your guides. Be bold and dare this grand adventure that is your own wondrous life.

How to Use this Book

The core intention of your Path of She journey of soul is to find your way home to the beauty of your Deep Self, the living ways of Nature, and the life-centered ethos of the sacred feminine. This momentous undertaking is the work of a lifetime, and you start, always, with wherever you are right now, trusting your life to lead the way.

This book guides you on your journey of soul across the eight Sabbats of the Wheel of the Year. In each Sabbat chapter, a Sabbat Mystery and Teaching share key themes, seasonal wisdom and illuminating gifts from Nature, the sacred feminine, and the God or Goddess for this potent celebration day. Guided Meditation and Inner and Outer Pathwork exercises help you engage the transformative powers of these seasonal themes, wisdom and gifts in service of your healing and personal growth. The Walk the Path section, at the end of each chapter, directs your continued exploration of the Sabbat lessons and pathwork.

As you engage these Sabbat materials across the seasons and apply them to your life, you gather precious knowledge, insights, experiences and skills that help you reclaim the lost pieces of your inner landscape, life story and authentic humanity, and reconnect with Nature, your Deep Self and the sacred feminine.

There is no right or wrong way to make this journey of soul. The writings and exercises in these pages are catalysts to help you dive deep into your own story and pathwork. Be clear in your intention, commit to your process, pay attention and do your best. Then trust that whatever shows up is your work of soul.

Though this book is designed to take you through a full cycle of the Sabbats, you can also use its contents in whatever way best serves your personal needs and inspirations: as a yearlong journey of soul across the seasons; an in-depth exploration of a specific Sabbat, teaching or exercise; or a resource for your spiritual practice and Sabbat celebrations.

Whatever you choose, remember that paganism is not just about ideas and beliefs, it's about stepping outside of the boundaries of everyday reality and your old stories and patterns, and stepping into full-bodied experiences of what else is true and possible. Show up to the Sabbat teachings and tasks — grounded, empty, curious and open to change — and life will gift you with the natural and spiritual realm encounters, lost parts of your Deep Self and life story, and soul lessons that will best serve your healing and growth.

In everything you do, truly make this work your own. Adjust the seasonal descriptions in the text to best reflect how Nature reveals itself in your part of the world, and how you best connect with the wild beauty around you. Read each meditation over and adapt its symbols and steps to create your own Sabbat meditation. Dedicate a time and space for your Sabbat activities. Use a special journal or sketchbook to record your pathwork. Continue your explorations through your favorite creative process: journaling, poetry, dance, painting or any other expressive practice.

Self-care and self-responsibility are key elements of your Sabbat journey, especially in the seasons that take you into the darkness and shadow sides of your inner landscape, life story and our collective humanity. Remember that you are the master of your own journey, and that you do your work in alignment with your highest good and at the depth that is right for you.

The materials in this book are in no way meant to replace therapy or other professional support. If you find yourself dealing with difficult, painful or disruptive parts of your life story and pathwork, step back and assess whether you are ready for this work. If you choose to proceed, ensure you have the personal and professional resources you need to do your pathwork safely, compassionately and wisely.

Most important, remember that you are on a journey fueled by a fierce, unrelenting love that flows through all of Creation — a vast, shining love that calls you home, always, to its life-giving embrace. It is this love, inside of you, outside of you, that can hold, guide and transform you through the seasons of your life, and that helps you become ever more deeply, beautifully your Self.

I am honored to walk this Path with you!

Fall Equinox

Always at the Fall Equinox,
the sacred dark opens portals
that beckon you,
beyond your known world
into their mysterious depths,
to seek out the next cycle
on your journey of soul.

A new cycle on your journey of soul begins at the Fall Equinox. The mysteries of the dark and the ways of the natural realm beckon, calling you to step beyond the outer edge of your known world in search of the focus of your healing and personal growth pathwork for the months to come.

In the natural realm, the Fall Equinox marks a moment of balance between light and dark before the land retreats from the sunlit munificence of Summer into the cold sleep of Winter. Living things begin to slow down and turn inward as darkness waxes, days shorten and temperatures drop. Nature gifts us with a final display of color in the scarlet-red, pumpkin-orange and golden-yellow of autumn leaves before trees settle into their bare-branch repose.

In rural communities, the bounty of late harvest crops is celebrated with Fall Fairs and Harvest Festivals. The cornucopia is filled with apples, grapes, gourds and root vegetables. These celebrations find their roots in our agrarian past when our ancestors gathered in their foodstuff in preparation for Winter, and offered up their gratitude for the plenitude of the land.

Another cycle begins in the potent embrace of the descending dark. Though our modern sensibilities are disconnected from these primal patterns and mysteries, tales of the Goddess from our ancient past preserve these mystery teachings for us.

At the Fall Equinox, it is the Goddess Persephone, with Her story of descent into the Underworld, who guides your journey of soul. Though we best know the Greek version of this myth, with Persephone as helpless victim and Hades as ruthless kidnapper, Her story arises from more ancient, sacred feminine origins. In keeping with these older mythic roots, Persephone travels to the realm of the sacred dark, by Her own choice and free will, in search of the missing half of Her nature and Her spiritual evolution.

Like Persephone, you are seeking the missing parts of your Deep Self and authentic humanity on your journey of soul. Your Deep Self holds your spiritual essence and soul-sourced beauty and gifts. Your authentic humanity arises out of a potent confluence of the light and dark, and the feminine and masculine aspects of human nature, and your connection to these omnipresent energies in the natural world.

We have lost our connection to the sacred feminine and the sacred dark, and from this tear in the fabric of our humanity, a great imbalance and discord arise in our personal lives and human society. Yet what has been lost can be re-found.

At the Fall Equinox, the natural world and Persephone's tale point the way. To find balance, you must turn off the lights, turn off your mind, turn off your busy-ness, and slow down, retreat inward and open yourself to the dark, feminine side of your nature. Like Persephone, you must forsake the sunlit realm and descend into the fertile, secrets ways of the Underworld that reside within your inner landscape and the mysteries that suffuse waking reality. A new cycle of healing and transformation, for yourself and our world, reaches out to you from the sacred dark.

A Sabbat Mystery
Persephone and the Ways of the Sacred Feminine

At the edge of the edge of the sunlit realm, where a rough-hewn stone stairway leads down into the velvety darkness of the Underworld, Persephone awaits you, still and silent, wrapped in a black cloak that rustles in a bone-chilling wind.

She is beautiful and fearsome, with penetrating, dark-blue eyes, pale skin, lips the rich red of pomegranate, and long, lustrous, ebony-brown hair. This is not the young maiden Goddess, alight with joy and innocence, that you may have read about in the ancient tales, but a regal being who has fully claimed Her place and sovereignty in the great weaving of life.

"Change is in the air," Persephone says after She has greeted you, "For millennia, humanity has rejected the ways of the sacred feminine and the powers of the sacred dark that reside within the Underworld. There is a grievous imbalance in your world that cuts you off from the natural cycles and powers of life, and your own whole/holy nature."

"Yet the season of humanity is turning and a great awakening is upon you. Your Deep Self is reaching for you, calling you to a life of soul, and drawing you back to my side and the lost ways of the sacred feminine."

She extends Her arm and you wrap your fingers in the soft, black folds of Her cloak. The space around you shimmers and morphs, and you find yourself transported to another time and place, looking out on a scene from when the world was fresh and new.

A younger version of Persephone plays in the meadow before you, picking flowers and smiling Her delight. Her face has the warm tones of skin kissed by sunlight and Her eyes are a lighter shade of blue gray.

"You see me here when I lived in the bright circle of my Mother Demeter's loving embrace," the older Persephone beside you says, "Life was very, very good. The green-growing realm was my playground and I wanted for nothing. Yet I was restless, always seeking the outer edge of things, hungry to know more, experience more, become more."

As you watch, the young Persephone wanders further and further from the meadow and the protective circle of Her Mother. Her light-hearted smile has been replaced by an intense focus, as if She is being drawn forward by a compelling, irresistible force.

A great fissure appears in the Earth at Her feet and a God-like being emerges. He emanates a powerful elixir of animal magnetism and ethereal beauty, as if He is equally woven of flesh and light. A piercing cold spreads outward from His body, withering the wildflowers and yellowing the leaves within reach of His frosty breath. Yet His somber, coal-black eyes are filled with tender warmth as He gazes down at the lovely Persephone.

"Hades," She whispers with a note of longing in Her voice, taking a tentative step in His direction.

"Come," He says, extending a hand to Her, "it is time for your awakening."

For a moment young Persephone pauses, looking over Her shoulder from where She came and then down into the inky darkness before Her. And in this moment, it's as if you are inside of Persephone, feeling the push and pull of Her trepidation and profound hunger in the face of this vast, unknown realm. A calm determination rises up from Her core, quieting Her fast-beating heart and steeling Her resolve. Then She slips Her hand into Hades's, a faint smile playing across Her lips, and the Earth closes over their heads, swallowing them whole.

The scene disappears and you are once more standing beside the older Persephone at the stone steps leading into the Underworld.

"Life never stands still," Persephone says, "Something inside of us seeks the edge of what we know in search of our deeper and greater becoming.

"No matter my worldly knowledge and gifts, and all the

lovely things that gave me joy and pleasure, I was incomplete in the sunlit realm of my Mother's world. The dark side of my feminine nature was missing, compelling me to descend into the Underworld, with Hades as my companion and guide, to find and awaken the dormant pieces of my whole/holy nature."

As Persephone speaks, the light fades from the sky and a profound stillness settles on the land. Fall is in the air and the natural world, like Persephone, has begun its descent into the mysteries of darkness.

"I tell you my story so you may know the ways of the sacred feminine," Persephone continues, "To seek the true power and nature of your Deep Self, you must step past the border of your known world into the depths of the Underworld that resides in the inner folds of your psyche and in the mysteries that underlie waking reality."

"When you brave the Underworld and travel its ways, you reclaim what has been lost, the sacred feminine and sacred dark, and you begin the hard, hard work of returning balance and wholeness to your life and world. Your journey will not be easy because the trials and revelations of the sacred dark are meant to test and teach you. And yet, if you follow in my footsteps and stay the course, healing and profound change will come.

"This journey of soul begins with wherever you are right now, at this moment. Whatever is ready to awaken in you waits for you in the sacred dark."

Persephone places Her hand on your chest, sending Her wise teachings into the core of your being. Her story is your story, the story of the turning of the seasons into Fall, and the story of the unfolding of our collective humanity. Always at the

Fall Equinox, the sacred darkness opens portals that beckon to a new cycle of healing and growth.

Then Persephone's touch and presence are gone. Yet you are not alone at the portal to the Underworld. He waits for you on the stone stairs, a magical messenger to guide your journey home to your Deep Self.

"Come," He says, His hand extended to you and His eyes brimming with tender warmth, "it is time for your awakening."

Take His hand, descend; the sacred darkness and your deepest becoming await you.

A Sabbat Teaching
The Illuminating Dark Path

Light and dark modulate the turning of the seasons in Nature. At the Fall Equinox, the wild realm responds to the increasing darkness of shorter, colder days by slowing down and retreating inward. Trees shed their leaves in a brilliant splash of autumn colors. Birds and squirrels stockpile seeds and nuts. Animals prepare for hibernation.

We humans invented the light bulb and suddenly the dark didn't hold much sway in our lives. Out of sync with the natural world, we ignore the impulse to slow down and turn inward with the increasing darkness, and we snap back into action at the end of Summer. By the Fall Equinox, we are full steam ahead in our everyday pursuits.

The light shines bright and we do whatever we want, whenever we want, disconnected from the rhythms of the living Earth. We think and act in the illuminated circle of the things that we can see, name and know, ignoring the mysteries and wonders that reside in the dark edges of our awareness.

The light shines bright, holding the frightening things in the dark at bay. In our modern world, we don't worry anymore about predatory animals with keen night vision. Yet still we fear the dark and project onto it the nasty contents of the toxic, destructive aspects of our human psyche and behavior.

The light shines bright and profound quiet, stillness and repose evade us. We no longer live as the other creatures on this planet, dialed into a seasonal clock that honors darkness equally to light, and the emergence of life from the mysteries of the dark.

The light shines bright but rather than finding our way, we lose it.

Thankfully the darkness we have rejected is still very much part of us. Yes it is clogged with the rejected and denied debris of our sorrow, pain, fears and dysfunction. And yes we have long forgotten how to travel its ways and dance with its powers. Though it may be daunting, still our journey of healing and transformation leads us back to the dark, both inside and outside of us.

And in this darkness, the things we hunger for most, the lost parts of our Deep Self and authentic humanity, await us: the sparkling jewels of our personal gifts and best qualities, mysteries long repressed and forgotten in the waking world, secret stories that can set us free, wondrous possibilities not yet imagined, and the natural cycles and instincts of our creature body.

On this Fall Equinox Sabbat, heed the call of the dark on your living flesh. Slow down and retreat inward to the mysteries of your inner darkness. Every new cycle begins here. Your journey home to your Deep Self emerges from here. Paradoxically, it is the dark that illuminates your path forward.

Guided Meditation
Descent Into the Sacred Dark

At the twilight hour on the Fall Equinox, when daylight gives way to the dark, settle into an open, meditative state in a private corner of your home. Close your eyes and place your hands on your belly. Breathe in and out, in and out, focusing your awareness on the movements of your belly with breath, rounding outward and flattening inward, slow, rhythmic, entrancing. Feel your whole body soften and relax with every inhale and exhale.

Draw your awareness inward, like turning all the lights out in your home and using a single candle to find your way in the darkness. Quiet your mind. Quiet the outside noises of the everyday world. Pay attention instead to the movements and sounds of your breath, slow in, slow out, slow in, slow out.

Imagine the changing season outside your doorstep. Visualize the quality of the light and darkness, and the altered appearance of the trees and plants. Smell the fall scents in the air and feel the change in temperature on your skin. Sense the presence of the descending darkness, calling the natural realm to retreat inward to stillness and rest.

Breathe these seasonal shifts into your body and inner world. Imagine them calling forth your own shifting seasons from the hidden places inside of you. Sense them drawing up the deep mysteries and hungers within you, and the lost parts of you longing for your conscious engagement. Every new cycle begins here, in the powerful embrace of the sacred dark.

Like Persephone, you must forsake the sunlit world of what you know and descend into the Underworld in search of the new cycle awakening within you. The guidance and answers you seek on your journey of soul await you there.

Take a few minutes to check in with your emotions before you begin your meditation journey. Whatever emotions arise, acknowledge them and then let them pass through you. If you experience fear or resistance, shift your attention back to your breath until you feel still and centered once more. From this grounded place, set the intention to only engage the pathwork that is right for you at this moment, and then let your fear and resistance slip away as well.

Focus your awareness inward and call forth the part of you that knows the ways of Persephone and the sacred dark. Open to your profound hunger to experience and become more, and to seek out the lost parts of your Deep Self and authentic humanity; here you will find your inner Persephone. Let this part of you lead the way, taking you to the outer edge of your known world to a portal with stairs that descend into the dark mysteries of the Underworld.

As you make your way to this portal, feel your feet solid on the ground and your breath and awareness centered within your inner core. Empty your mind, leaving behind any preconceived ideas or expectations you may have. You are traveling beyond what you know into the wondrous realm of what else is true and possible.

When you reach the portal, take in your surroundings and the magnetic draw of the energies emerging from the opening before you. Breathe deep of the magic of the Underworld. Be clear in your intention to do your pathwork in service of your greater becoming and in alignment with your highest good at this time.

Then summon up your courage and determination to follow in Persephone's footsteps, and respectfully ask the sacred dark to show you what you need to know at this turning of the Fall

Equinox, and where your journey of soul will take you next.

Someone appears on the step below you, a magical messenger come to guide your journey of soul. Take whatever time you need to connect, heart to heart and center to center, with this being who has especially shown up to support your pathwork. Speak your name and anything else you are inspired to share. Then reach for this messenger's hand and follow her/him into the Underworld.

As you descend the stairs, stay with your hunger and curiosity, empty and receptive; you can't discover anything new if you are too full of what you already know. Imagine that your magical messenger is leading you to the exact level of depth in the Underworld that will gift you with the experiences you need to understand and embrace the next cycle of your journey of soul.

When you reach the bottom of the stairs and step into the sacred dark, surrender yourself to your messenger and your own intuition and instincts, and see what comes to you. You may find yourself in a familiar setting from your adulthood or a vivid memory from childhood. Perhaps you will experience something more surreal, akin to a dream. Or you may receive guidance as a voice speaking inside of your head or body sensations and energies flowing through you.

There is no right way to do Underworld work; just open to whatever shows up, ask whatever questions come to you and be with your messenger, be with your inner Persephone, and be with the darkness. Let your explorations mend and deepen your connection with the sacred feminine and sacred dark. What has been lost can be refound and reclaimed in the depths of the Underworld.

When your work together feels complete, ask your messenger to guide you back to the foot of the stairs. Take a few minutes to solidify your connection, and to feel the rightness and goodness of the energy that flows between you. Drink in everything you have experienced together. As you say goodbye, be sure to express your heartfelt gratitude and to ask for your messenger's continued support as you embark on this new cycle of your journey of soul.

Your time in the sacred dark, for now, is complete. Ascend the stairs slowly and purposely. With each step, feel your experiences in the Underworld settle into your flesh and bones, and re-arrange your inner landscape in alignment with the profound roots of this new cycle awakening within you. Don't rush to solidify any of this into words or plans of action. The mysteries of the dark need time to percolate in your psyche.

As you step over the portal's threshold, you have returned to the sunlit realm of the world that you know. Feel this shift in energy from the dark back into the light. Let it register in your inner knowing and physical body so you will remember the embrace of the sacred dark when you encounter it again. Then bow to the Underworld, honor its beauty and place in your life and our world, and share your appreciation and gratitude.

Use your breath to ground your awareness in your physical form and bring you back to waking consciousness. Gently tap your body and say your name out loud. Open your eyes and connect with the darkness that has descended during your meditation.

Substantive, lasting change finds its source in the mysteries of the dark. So too your Underworld travels can be the beginning of a brave, new adventure of healing your soul and transforming your life. Let the experiences and insights that came to you in your meditation guide you in the months to come, leading you home to your greater becoming and the beauty and power of your Deep Self.

Inner Pathwork
Dark as Fear, Dark as Friend

The dark has been given a bad rap in our human world. Since we were children, we've been conditioned to see darkness as the repository of all things bad and scary. The worst aspects of our humanity are attributed to the dark; dark places are scenes of crime and violence; the dark recesses of our mind are where we stuff the things we want to forget and repress. Through our meaning-making and actions, we have made the dark something to fear.

What is the dark outside of our fear-based projections? It is the absence of light, a place where we cannot see clearly. It is the secret depths of our mind, the inner spaces in our body, and the hidden mysteries that permeate everyday consciousness. It is the gaping maw of death that swallows us at the end of our days. The dark is the unknown and the uncontrollable, a thing that cannot be domesticated or intellectually contained. These are the deeper reasons we fear the dark.

Darkness is a natural, essential element of life on Earth, and we can no more sever our connection to the dark then we can decide to do without oxygen. The dark invites us to turn our gaze inward to stillness, quiet and the wide, wild expanse of what else is true and possible. And it is here, beyond the edge of our known world, that we can find the lost parts of our Deep Self and authentic humanity that hold our true beauty and best gifts, and the repressed and forgotten pieces of our personal story in need of reclaiming, healing and transformation on our journey of soul.

On the Path of She, we embrace the dark as a friend and ally in our pathwork. Most of us have healing work to do before we can make this shift from fear to friend. The following activities can help you begin to explore, mend and deepen your relationship with the dark.

Take out a piece of paper and set an alarm for twenty minutes. Write: "The Dark" at the top of the page, and then use the allotted time to record your word associations, thoughts and feelings about the dark. Don't think, just write.

Then set the alarm for another twenty minutes. Write: "What else is true?" at the top of the page. Take a few deep breaths to relax and ground yourself in your body. Shift to a place of curiosity and wonder about what else could be true about the dark. Then let the dark speak to you through your writing in the allotted time. Again don't think, just write.

That night spend twenty minutes alone in the dark. If you live somewhere rural, with no street lights, do this outside. If not, go to a quiet room in your home where no one will disturb you and turn out the lights. See what arises in you — thoughts, associations, sensations and feelings — as you experience the dark. If you find yourself afraid, blocked or solely focusing on the negative, take a few deep breaths and shift into your curiosity about what else is true. Open to the idea of the dark as your ally and see what comes to you.

For the next few days, reflect on your writings and experiences. How do you relate to the dark? Are your reactions primarily negative, positive or a mix of both? How has the mainstream culture influenced your reactions? Has anything happened to you personally that has affected your relationship with the dark? What did the dark teach you when you shifted to a place of curiosity? How can the dark be your ally in your pathwork?

Make it part of your regular personal practice to pay attention to your relationship to the dark.

Recognize and challenge your fears and negative projections. Spend quiet, meditative time in the darkness, opening to its mysteries and gifts. Honor and welcome the lost parts of your Deep Self, authentic humanity and life story that the dark returns to you. Gently, and with a conscious, supported process, explore and heal whatever hurts arise from your inner darkness.

You don't need to rush this process. You can't change your attitudes or heal your hurtful experiences overnight, nor can you directly alter our cultural biases about the dark. But you can choose to mend and reclaim your natural, balanced connection to the dark. Start by accepting wherever you are in your relationship with the dark right now. Name your projections and fears, acknowledge that the dark is what it is, outside of your biases, and commit to making the dark your friend and ally on your journey of soul.

Outer Pathwork
A Shift In Seasons

Every Fall Equinox, I feel the tug of the change of seasons on my flesh: the hint of frost, the softer light, the yellowing leaves and the musty smell of the forest floor. I don an extra layer of clothing and eye the woodstove, tempted to light a fire to fend off the chill. The days are getting shorter, and where I live the sky will soon take on a near-constant, overcast hue of charcoal gray, offering up copious amounts of rain and a damp cold that settles into my bones.

And with the Fall season, like the natural world, I invariably turn my attention inward. Dreams and insights come to me, speaking to the matters most pressing to my Deep Self and the emerging focus of my healing and growth in the next cycle of my journey of soul.

No matter our level of conscious awareness of these things, we absorb and respond to the physical and energetic turnings of the seasons. Our body, with its fleshy matter and creature sensibilities, is not separate from the natural world. And the seasons of our spiritual journey adhere to the same primal mysteries that underlie the outer shifts in Nature.

Take some time out of your busy life to experience and heed the seasonal shift of the Fall Equinox in your part of the world. Go for a walk in a green space and open your senses to the natural realm. What do you see? Smell? Hear? Feel? How is the light different from a month ago? What do you notice about the air temperature and scents? What is happening to the plants and trees? What are the bugs, birds and animals doing?

Bring this same open awareness to the human and urban landscapes around you. Notice the dress, body language and activities of the people you cross paths with. How are things different from last month? How do these changes relate to Fall's seasonal shift? Are they connected or disconnected from Nature's inner retreat in response to the increasing darkness and shorter, colder days?

When you return home from your awareness outings, spend time in inner reflection. Imagine breathing your encounters with the natural and human realms into your body, and feel them draw forth the seasonal shift in your own life. What adjustments do you make in your routines, activities and priorities at this time of year? How connected or disconnected are you from the seasonal shift in the natural world? What new opportunities and challenges have come your way? What matters to you and has your attention? What spiritual and interpersonal issues and opportunities are up for you? What personal changes do these things suggest? Take a measure of your emotional state. Are you happy, excited, depressed, stressed, fearful or experiencing some other emotion? How is this different than a month ago?

Follow Nature's example by drawing your awareness deeper into your inner landscape.

As with the guided meditation, track the sounds and sensations of your breath until your body relaxes and your mind becomes quiet. Imagine anchoring your conscious focus in the core of your being. From this deep, soul-level place, ask yourself: what new cycle is beginning on my journey of soul? What is the primary focus of my pathwork for the coming months?

Let the answers come to you in words, sensations and images, sourced from the experiences and encounters from your Fall Equinox meditation and this outer pathwork exercise. Be in a place of openness and ease, letting the questions percolate within you, and trust that insights and answers will come when they are ready and ripe.

Though these exercises may seem simple, they suggest a personal practice of reflection and conscious engagement of your spiritual journey in keeping with the physical and energetic shifts in the natural world, and their reflective shifts in the human realm. So without, so within; as the seasons turn, so do the focus and patterns of your life and pathwork. To observe and experience this profound truth in the unfolding of your own life is to reclaim what has been lost: your primal, innate connection to the cycles and mysteries of our Earth home.

Walk the Path
New Beginnings and Radical Self-Care

The Fall Equinox calls you to new beginnings. In your

meditation, you descended into the Underworld in search of guidance on the new, emerging cycle of your journey of soul. Through your meditation, and in your inner and outer pathwork, you explored and deepened your relationship with the sacred feminine, the sacred dark and the seasonal turnings of Nature.

This kind of pathwork may be new to you, or you may be building upon your existing spiritual practice. Regardless of your experience level, the Fall Equinox reminds you to slow down, turn your awareness inward, and step beyond what you know in search of the new cycle of healing and growth that reaches to you from the sacred dark, within and without. In the weeks that follow, continue to let the ways of the sacred feminine and sacred dark help you gain greater clarity on where your journey of soul is taking you next.

Heed the directives of your inner landscape that come through your dreams, intuition and sudden insights. What is shifting inside of you will also shift things on the outside.

Notice anything unusual, unexpected or attention grabbing in your everyday life. Bring greater awareness to any challenges or positive changes you are facing. Look for patterns and themes that link these inner and outer occurrences. Sense your gut responses, either of attraction or repulsion.

Gather these clues to you, building on the insights you gained through your meditation and outer pathwork exercise, to develop a clearer understanding of the focus and intent of your new cycle of healing and growth. But don't push for concrete, tidy conclusions or jump into action.

At the Fall Equinox, the natural world shifts into a slower, inward-focused state. You can emulate this in your pathwork by remaining open and fluid in your personal explorations, and by making time for introspection and meditation. Remember to step past the outer edges of your usual patterns of thoughts and behavior, and to embrace the sacred dark, inner and outer, as your friend and ally that can guide your pathwork and help you take your life in new directions.

Persephone's tale tells us that our journey of soul won't be easy. As you continue to mend and deepen your relationship with the sacred feminine and sacred dark, and to engage the pathwork that arises out of your personal darkness, you will encounter the painful along with the beautiful. But you don't have to rush headlong into the challenging contents of your inner landscape, nor of our collective dark places. Set the intention to travel slowly, gently and compassionately on your journey of soul, only taking on pathwork that you are ready for.

Radical self-care is an essential complimentary practice to your pathwork. Cultivate a high degree of self-responsibility and care to ensure that you make safe, wise choices for yourself at each step on your spiritual journey.

Tend to your body and your soul. Do things that give you joy, peace and satisfaction. At any time, if you touch painful or difficult parts of your story, check in with yourself and make sure this is work you are ready for. And always ensure you have the personal and professional resources you need to safely and wisely facilitate your healing process. On your journey of soul, you can't avoid the bumpy parts, but you can hold and support these parts from a place of radical self-care and love.

And remember always that what you seek is nothing less than the lost beauty and power of your Deep Self and authentic humanity. Cycle by cycle, season by season, step by step, you return balance and wholeness to your life and our world as you journey home to your Self.

Samhain

The Crossroads
call to you at Samhain.
A place of endings
that promise new beginnings,
where your destiny is woven
by the choices
you make.

Your journey of soul brings you face-to-face with profound endings and weighty choice making at Samhain. Nature's death-like state and the potent mysteries of Samhain draw you into the deep roots of your spiritual journey as you embark on a new cycle of healing and personal growth.

Nature makes its final transitions into its winter mode of dormancy at Samhain. The outer appearance of things changes dramatically. Deciduous trees shed the last of their leaves. Some plants and animals die. Others alter their life patterns, slowing down their metabolism, putting on a thick winter covering, and hibernating. Sleep and stillness spread across the wild landscape.

Our human realm also turns its awareness toward death and endings. The final crops of the season are harvested. Cultures around the world celebrate and honor their beloved ancestors at this time of year. Halloween traditions and imagery harken back to the pagan belief that the veil between the worlds is thin at Samhain, allowing for communion between the living and the dead.

Death on your journey of soul is not about physical death, but about soul-sourced, life-changing endings. And this can very much feel like death, stirring up your pain, sorrow, fear and resistance.

Yet endings are not what they appear to be. The death-like state of Nature at Samhain is an illusion. Yes there is physical death in the wild world, but there is also gestating new life. Underneath the outer dormancy, life is present, resting and rejuvenating in preparation for the glorious rebirth of Spring.

So too the profound endings that arise as you embark on a new cycle of your journey of soul contain the promise of new beginnings. And like the natural world retreating deeper into darkness at Samhain, your journey takes you deeper into the mysteries of the sacred dark.

Between the worlds, in the heart of the sacred dark, the Goddess Hecate stands at Her crossroads, offering the beacon of Her shining love-light and Crone wisdom to guide you in this season of life-changing endings.

Hecate is not the evil cartoon hag of Halloween and Hollywood movies, nor the corrupter of men portrayed in Shakespeare's Macbeth. She is more primal and powerful than the Goddess that comes to us through Greek mythology, though Her crossroads magic is preserved in these mythic accounts.

Hecate is the Dark Mother who has been with us from the very beginning of our species's birth from the starlit realm into our flesh and blood form. And She has guided us always in the ways and mysteries of the sacred feminine, and in the trials and triumphs of our spiritual evolution.

At Samhain, your journey of soul leads you to Hecate's crossroads in search of the deepest roots of your personal healing and spiritual evolution.

Her crossroads can reveal many things, from the critical juncture we collectively face in these Great Turning times of societal upheaval and transformation, to the profound endings and new beginnings that will guide your personal pathwork in the months to come.

In Hecate's loving presence and the potent mysteries of Samhain, you can choose your path forward into Her life-centered ways and your greater becoming. And in this choice making, you can naturally play your part in the positive, evolutionary momentum we can create together in these Great Turning times.

A Sabbat Mystery
Hecate and the Crossroads of Choice

At Samhain, when the veil between the worlds is thin and the mysteries of the sacred dark permeate the mundane world, Hecate calls to us. Never before has Her voice been so loud, so urgent. She speaks to us not only in our dreams and ritual magic, but also in the stark language of wildly erratic weather patterns, dying oceans and barren lands, and in the cold despair and hungry hopes of our warm, beating heart.

It`s not easy to heed Her call. She raises our own spectral fears about the fate of our human society and planet home. Environmentally, socially, politically and spiritually, we are destroying the fabric of our physical and social world. We have reached a critical tipping point, and if we continue on this trajectory, things are not going to end well.

But how do we change? How do we shift from denial, apathy and despair into a place of hope and inspiration? How do we turn this destructive momentum into an evolutionary, birthing moment? And what is our personal part in weaving a better world into being?

"Come to my crossroads," Hecate whispers on the wind, "Come and you will find the answers you seek."

Take a deep breath, summon up your courage and say, "Yes, Hecate, I am coming. Guide me to your crossroads."

In the world between the worlds, where the mysteries lie in wait, you will find Hecate. She appears before you in Her Crone form, with a thick mane of moonlight-silver hair and intense, amethyst eyes that shine bright with Her ageless presence. She wears a cloak of midnight black that shimmers as She moves, as if brushed with starlight. An aura of light surrounds Her, a way-showing beacon in the enveloping darkness to guide travelers to Her crossroads. Her arms open wide to welcome you, casting a circle of illumination that draws you into its center.

With a sweep of Her hands, two paths appear before you.

To the left is a neglected path, overgrown with the luscious fecundity of the wild realm. Memories arise within you of the feral innocence of childhood with its simple pleasures of play and wonder in your dance with the outer world. And beneath this, older, ancestral memories percolate, of a time when humanity lived in loving, sensual communion with the powers and mysteries of the Mother Earth.

To the right is a paved-over surface that obscures any trace of the living land under an unforgiving, tar-black sheen. This path exudes a deadness that lays bare the tear in our human psyche from the natural world and our Deep Self, and echoes with the keening pain of our battered souls and broken hearts.

"Behold the crossroads of these Great Turning times, where humanity faces a critical, precarious juncture in its spiritual evolution," Hecate says, *"Before you are two ways of living and dreaming."*

"One path holds the good dream of humanity where you walk the Earth in accordance with my life-centered ways and your best nature of love, generosity and communion with others. The second path holds the bad dream where your worst instincts of dominion, fear and greed lay barren the wild realm and the heart of your human society. It is this second path, reeking devastation on the living world, that rules humankind.

"Both of these paths exist inside of you and in your greater society. Humanity is neither good nor bad, but a complex weaving that includes the best and worst of your nature."

With another sweep of Her hands, the two paths merge into

one.

"This is my middle path," Hecate says," it holds the opposing paths of the good and bad dream of humanity. A mirror path exists inside of you that contains the joy and sorrow, and beauty and wounding of your life story.

"To transform yourself and your world, you must walk this middle path. To travel its ways is to accept and take responsibility for all that you are and all that you have experienced, and from this greater awareness choose whether the good or bad dream of humanity will hold sway in the core of your being. You must choose whether love or fear will rule you.

"Love is the way forward for you and your human kin — love that can hold and heal the sorrow and wounding that burden your soul and the world soul — love that chooses generosity over greed, and communion over dominion — love that can turn the destructive momentum that threatens this world into a positive, new beginning. This love is my way, the way of the sacred feminine, that is awakening within you and leading you home to your Deep Self and a better world."

As Hecate speaks, the light that emanates from Her being shines brighter and brighter. This wondrous luminosity is the very love that She speaks of, offering a beacon of guidance and hope in these turbulent, Great Turning times. Hecate, the sacred feminine, all life on this stunning Earth, your life, are woven of this love.

Hecate turns to you, taking your hands and squeezing them tight.

"Time is running out. Do not turn away," She says, "By your choices, and those of your human kin, your destiny and that of your Earth home will be decided."

She folds Her arms inward, drawing Her brilliant light back into Her body until She is gone, and you find yourself alone under a star-studded sky. Your hands still tingle from Her touch, and the responsibility She has bequeathed to you shines strong and bright within you.

After the crossroads vision is done, the real magic begins. With your every thought, every word, every action, you choose which path your life serves, and the kind of world you want to create. Never have the stakes been higher; life as we know it hangs in the balance. To change this world, you must start with yourself.

A Sabbat Teaching
Born Into Life, Born Into Death

The natural world and our human psyche turn toward the mysteries of death at Samhain. Cold and darkness descend upon the land, and the wild world shifts into decay and a death-like sleep. In many cultures, this time of year is marked by offerings and rituals to honor the dead, our beloved ancestors.

Usually we don't like to think about death. Most of us run as fast as we can from the frightening specter that decline and death conjure in us. It is the ultimate irony that the moment we are born into life, with our very first breath, we are also born into death. And we must live every moment, every breath, knowing that we will die, and that everything around us, all that we love and cherish, will eventually come to decay, to death, to dust.

Samhain teaches us that there is no hiding from death. It comes in the falling of leaves, the lengthening darkness and the cold grip of Winter. It comes in our remembrances of our beloved ancestors who have passed on. It comes in the wrenching of our heart as we witness a dear one slip from this world into the next. It comes with the graying at our temples, the sagging of our flesh and the unstoppable march toward our last breath.

And death comes with gifts in hand if we have the courage to show up raw and naked to our pain, losses and fears.

Death strips us to the basics:
that every breath is a miracle not to be wasted;
that each person, creature and life form, is
worthy, precious, sacred;
that life is oh so hard and oh so exquisite;
that pain and loss help us remember what we
cherish most;
and that love, at the end of all things, is what
remains.

Love is death's most precious gift to us. Love, not money, possessions, career, social esteem and the many other alluring outer trappings of life, is the balm that soothes us in the face of death. Love is what connects us to those who have passed on. Love calls us to reach out and hold each other in our grief. Love is what joins us, heart to heart and soul to soul, to another. Love is our best offering from our Deep Self to the world.

Samhain is a time to contemplate the mysteries of death, not from a place of fear and resistance, but from an acceptance of death as a teacher and guide for the living. Yes we are born into life and born into death, and it is this very, inescapable fact that makes every moment so precious, fragile and bittersweet beautiful.

Death isn't a summons to fear, it is an invitation to love, deeply, wildly, joyfully. And when death seeks us out at the end of our days, let our last breath be a prayer to love.

Guided Meditation
Powerful Choices for Powerful Times

On Samhain eve, in the pitch blackness of deep night, light a single candle in a quiet, private space in your home. Empty your mind, relax your body and let your eyes adjust to the near-dark of the candlelit room. Bring your awareness to the movements of your body with your breath. Feel the widening of your rib cage and rounding of your belly on the in-breath, and the compressing of your chest and belly on the out-breath. Track the slow, sensuous rhythm of your inhales and exhales, savoring each breath, until you feel anchored and fully present in your living flesh.

Open yourself to the energies of the natural world as it transits into its winter state of death and dormancy. Sense the withdrawal of energy inward to darkness and stillness, the falling away of leaves, the slowing metabolism of birds and beasts, and the sleeping life force within the barren landscape.

Breathe these wild realm energies into your body. Follow them inward to the dark stillness of your inner core. Tap into the deep roots of your spiritual journey that give rise to your soul-sourced impulse to reclaim your Deep Self and the best qualities of your humanity. Align yourself with the momentous shifts of the Great Turning that are calling you back to the love- and life-centered ethos of the sacred feminine. Then ask yourself: what is ending in my life? What death moment am I facing as I embark upon a new cycle on my journey of soul?

In this self-reflection, remember that life is a constant cycle of death and new beginnings — in the shifting of the seasons, the turning of day into night, and the rising and falling of your breath — in the consciously chosen and outwardly imposed losses and endings of your day-to-day life — in the suffering and passing of a loved one, and in your own fragile mortality, mapped out in the inevitable morphing of your physical form.

Surrender to your own constant cycle of endings and new beginnings, and be present to the personal change that is emerging for you at this time.

When you find the parts of your life that are ending and calling for your conscious engagement, speak them out loud to the listening darkness, and state your intention to travel to Hecate's crossroads to seek out Her guidance. Then imagine a path appearing at your feet that will lead to the heart of the sacred dark, between the worlds, where Hecate awaits you.

Fully inhabit each footstep as you walk this path toward Hecate. Know that you are consciously choosing to work crossroads magic with Her on this Sabbat night when the veil between the worlds is thin. You are the master of this journey, taking your destiny in your own hands and choosing to travel as deep and as far as is right for you at this moment.

See Hecate's luminescent form before you in the ebony darkness and close the distance between you. Take a few moments to connect with Hecate. What does She look like? How does it feel to be in Her presence? What words of welcome does She share? What words do you speak in return?

Let Hecate place Her hand upon your solar plexus. Commune with Her in the rich, dark stillness of your inner core, sharing the endings that are arising within you and the soul-sourced roots of your impetus for change.

With a sweep of Her hands, two paths appear, intersecting diagonally at your feet. This is your personal crossroads, unique from any other individual or any other season in your life. One path holds the stories and energies of your life as it is, and the other the life your journey of soul is calling you to. Here you can find everything you need to make wise, soulful choices in this death moment of shifting into a new cycle of healing and personal growth.

Step onto each path in turn and let it fill you with the parts of your life story that are woven into this death moment: what must end and what will emerge in its place, your fears and longings, and your doubts and hopes. Let yourself feel everything, know everything, for Hecate's is the middle path that calls you to be big, wise and powerful enough to embrace the full breadth, the good and the bad, of your life story.

Yet also practice self-care. If at any time you feel overwhelmed by the information and insights coming to you, remember that you are master of this journey and can choose how deep you want to engage your crossroads magic at this time.

As you return to the space between the crossroads, it is time to choose how you will respond to this particular death moment, and how to conceive and engage change itself.

Change, like death and endings, is inevitable. But how you engage the inevitable when it shows up on your doorstep is your choice.

You can choose to see change as your enemy or your teacher. You can choose to embrace the lessons and new beginnings offered by the endings of this death moment, or to let fear and resistance rule you and chain you to the path of your life as it is.

Take several slow, deep breaths and fill yourself with the shining light of Hecate's love. Feel the power and beauty of this love that can brave profound, life-changing endings, and can hold and heal the sorrow, wounding, joy and beauty of your life story and pathwork. This same love is inside of you, supporting and guiding your journey of soul.

Then ask yourself: am I ready to walk Hecate's middle path, consciously engaging all that I've been shown and all that I am in service of this transformational death moment? What endings am I willing to embrace? Will I let love and my best instincts guide my journey of soul? Be brave, choose wisely; these are powerful times requiring powerful choices.

Your time at Hecate's crossroads is drawing to a close. Look into Her eyes and acknowledge Her for who She truly is: the Dark Mother who knows you, loves you and is here, always, to guide you in these challenging ending moments on your journey through life. Offer Her your heartfelt gratitude as you bid Her farewell. Then use your breath to bring yourself back into your physical body and waking reality.

Blow out the candle and sit, quiet and still, within the enveloping darkness. This too is a crossroads moment, as is each breath and each moment that follows, because change comes to you in the little and big ways that mark your passage through time and space. In each of these moments, with every thought, word and action, you get to choose how to spend this precious offering that is your life. And by your choices, your destiny and that of our Earth home are woven.

Inner Pathwork
Love as a Guide to Fear

In these Great Turning times of momentous personal and social transformation, Hecate asks us which path will hold sway in our life: the bad dream with dominion and destruction as its ethos, or the good dream centered in Her life-affirming ways and our best nature. Will love or fear rule over our spiritual path?

Hecate doesn't ask us this question as a dualistic, either-or choice between fear or love. Instead, She calls us to walk Her middle path that embraces all that we are, with love, not fear, as our guide. In practice, this means that instead of repressing or banishing fear, we learn to work with our fear from a place of love.

When we travel a spiritual path of reclaiming our Deep Self, we are inviting profound endings and new beginnings into our life. And when we engage this kind of soul-deep, transformative change, our natural responses are going to include fear and resistance to anything that challenges the status quo in our life.

Fear typically shows up as a bullying, blocking energy that attempts to corral and control our beliefs, thoughts and actions. We have three fundamental choices in relation to our fears: submit, combat or step to one side. With the first two choices, submit or combat, fear is still controlling and defining the situation and our responses. In other words, fear is still ruling our life.

When love guides our spiritual path, we make the third choice, stepping to one side of fear's story and game. Love, in this context, is not an emotional state but an energetic imperative that is the beating heart of the sacred feminine; it is the primal desire of life to seek out, create and nurture life. With love as our guide, we have compassion and respect for our fear-based impulses, but we do not let fear delimit and truncate our pathwork of healing and personal growth.

Practice this third choice for yourself. For the focus of this exercise, pick a part of your life that makes you feel blocked and fearful. This can be something new related to your Samhain meditation around endings and new beginnings, or a recurring pattern or circumstance where you feel stuck and stressed.

Start by imagining yourself in this situation and let yourself experience the fear-based thoughts, emotions and body responses that come up for you. Notice any narrow line of thought that fixates your attention and limits your options and choice making. Don't analyze or problem solve, just be present to the voice and content of your fear response.

Let this go; empty your mind and use your awareness of the sounds and sensations of your body with breath to relax and ground. Place your hands on your solar plexus and focus your attention on the movements and energy beneath your palms.

When you feel still and empty, imagine stepping outside of your current way of thinking and engaging this situation, and widen your awareness beyond your fear-based thoughts and responses. Then ask: what else is true in this situation?

Let the answer come to you as energy and sensations, as if you are immersing yourself in a larger pool of information and potential, a place of being rather than knowing, beyond the limitations of mind and spoken words. Words, images or insights may come to you, but more important is the feeling of expanding and relaxing into what else is true and possible. You are loosening the threads that bind you to your entrenched patterns of thought and response, and letting in the transformative energies of new possibilities. Drink in these energies and let them infuse and inform your inner landscape.

As a last step, use your breath to come back to that still, empty place inside of you. When you feel centered, welcome your fear into this inner space as an ally in your change process. Look beneath fear's resistance and blocking tactics, and see what gifts of information and insights fear has to offer, such as: practical considerations that can help you make wise, balanced choices; sensitive, challenging parts of your psyche and life story that need extra, loving attention in your pathwork; or outer sources of reaction and resistance that need to be addressed.

When this communion feels complete, use your breath to come back to normal, waking reality. Stay in an open, receptive state of mind in relation to this situation and notice what further insights and information come to you in the days and weeks that follow. Don't jump to problem solving and action. Trust that resolution and right action will naturally come to you when the time and circumstances are right.

The process you have just experienced is Hecate's middle path. Your intention in this process is not primarily one of resolving the problematic situation and your associated fears, but more of being with your fears from the expansive space of what else is true and possible, and with the recognition of your fear as an ally with valuable information to share. With love as your guide, fear and the greater possibilities beyond fear both inform your journey of soul, providing you with insights and gifts that help you compassionately and wisely walk the path of your greater becoming.

Outer Pathwork
The Magic Cup of the Good

One Samhain, the very real, ever-mysterious presence of death descended upon my local community. A dear, precious friend was dying of cancer, and a small group of us gathered to support her and her family.

While I was visiting the hospital, another beloved friend joined us. The moment she entered the room, it was as if the sun had come out and pushed away the shadows for a little while. She smiled, bent to kiss our sick friend, and then settled into a chair across from me. She coaxed us to smile, laugh and share outrageous stories unfit for polite conversation, but delightful all the same. She brought with her a story of her young daughter who had dressed from head to foot in pink this school day in defiance of another girl who had declared pink evil. Her daughter, though only of elementary school age, would not allow someone to vilify something as dear to her as the color pink, the color of love. Then my friend left us to go on a love date with her husband — a perfect remedy for her aching heart.

It came to me after this hospital visit that our souls deeply need sunshine, goodness, humor and stories of courageous, young girls fighting for the color of love when faced with suffering and devastating loss.

Love, laughter, joy, goodness, wonder, delight, these are life's best gifts to us, to be savored in the moment and to be sourced as a balm to our inevitable sorrows and hardships.

Spend the next week gathering up all that is good in your life. Imagine that you have an inner magic cup in which you can pour your wondrous remembrances and best qualities: your stories of overcoming adversity and of shining your brightest; your happiest and most powerful experiences; the smiling faces of your children and loving family, your best friends, loudest cheerleaders and personal champions; your everyday heroes and the stories that inspire you; your favorite food, flower and place to be in the wild; your first love and current beloved, and every toe-curling orgasm that has ever rocked your body.

Whatever comes to you, clasp it to your heart, savor it and then pour its energy into your magic cup. Don't worry whether the cup will overflow; it is bottomless — the more juice, joy and love you pour in, the deeper and wider it gets.

At Samhain, we are called to consciously acknowledge and embrace the many faces of death. Death is our omnipresent companion in the small and big endings that mark our life's transitions, in the transformative change we must individually and collectively embrace to mend our human, destructive ways, and in the inevitable passing that waits for us at the end of our days. As you contemplate the soul-sourced endings that are arising for you this Samhain and the mysteries of death that infuse this season, remember that death and death-like endings have many gifts to offer, the most profound being our ability to expand our capacity for love, goodness and joy.

Make it a new habit to fill up your magic cup of goodness. Every day, whether life is blessing you or beating you down, you can fill up this magic cup because there is sunshine and beauty in every moment. Even when your heart is so raw and torn up that you cannot see past your pain and suffering, someone or something will come into the room and push away the shadows, even if just for a little while.

Walk the Path
Change Yourself, Change Our World

Your journey of soul at Samhain takes you to the heart of the sacred dark, to Hecate's crossroads between the worlds, in search of Her guidance and wisdom in these powerful, Great Turning times. In the weeks that follow, let your Samhain experiences and insights percolate within you, helping you understand and assess the endings you face as you embark upon a new cycle of healing and personal growth.

Use the following questions to continue your explorations and to bring additional direction to your spiritual journey: What do you want to commit your life to? How do you want to change in the following year? What endings do these changes require? Why are these changes and endings essential? What new possibilities would open for you?

Where there are core, rock-your-world endings, there is going to be fear. Rather than letting fear rule you, remember Hecate's middle path and use the inner pathwork process of letting love be your guide on your spiritual journey. Ask yourself: what else is true and possible beyond fear's story and game? And make fear your ally. Practice this process whenever your fear and resistance arise. Become a master at working with your fear from a place of love.

The Three Fold Law is a tenet held by some Wiccans and Pagans that says: whatever you do, for good or for ill, returns to you three times.

On one level, this can be seen as a pagan form of karma and an edict to promote positive magic. But on a deeper level, the Three Fold Law reminds us that we are not independent, separate entities, but part of a vast, interdependent web of life, and that every thought, choice and action we take, for good or for ill, is amplified beyond us and ultimately returns to us.

As part of assessing your individual process of endings and personal change, think about the social, political, environmental and spiritual aspects of your everyday way of living, and how they need to transform to bring about positive, sustainable change for the planet and for human society. Explore the beliefs that underlie your patterns of thought, choice and action. Consider the wider impact of your beliefs and choices beyond your individual life. What kind of world are you helping to create?

Take a break from this self-reflection and spend some time outside, communing with the still, bare splendor of Nature. Though death appears to have taken hold of the wild realm, new life is gestating in the dark belly of the land. So too your death-like endings hold the promise of new, life-serving beginnings.

Do not run from these death moments. Instead, let the inevitability of death remind you to live as if every moment matters, and to love with a wild, joyful abandon, knowing that love is death's best gift to you, and your best gift to the world.

Fill yourself with slow, deep breaths of the crisp, cold air. Listen to the steady rhythm of your heartbeat. Feel the warmth rising from your core. Pour all these wonderful blessings, and the million other ways it is good to be alive, into your magic cup. This is your precious, fragile, beautiful life, so choose wisely, love deeply and give your very best to yourself and others. Let these simple things guide your journey of soul, and profound transformation will come. Change yourself and you will change our world.

WINTER SOLSTICE

In the deepest dark
of Winter Solstice eve,
the light of a new dawn is born.
So too the depth
of your wounding
births forth the shining light
of your true beauty.

A t the Winter Solstice, your journey of soul takes you deep into the belly of the dark in search of the new beginnings ready to be born from the seeds of your beauty and wounding. In this essential work, you embrace the primal mysteries of darkness and light, and death and rebirth, as revealed in the ways of Nature, ancient Goddess tales and the turning seasons of our humanity.

Winter has taken hold of the wild realm, with the dark cloak of Nature gathered tight around the sleeping land. Daylight hours have diminished, reaching the point of the longest night as the solar year comes to its end. For a brief time, it appears as if the sun itself is standing still and night reigns over day. And then the wheel turns, shifting the balance to the returning light, with its promise of renewal and rebirth.

In our human world, this is a season of festive gatherings and gift giving, perhaps because we need the joy and comfort of each other's company as a solace to the heavy weight of the darkness on our hearts and psyche. The celebration of light and the miracle of rebirth are common themes in our holiday stories and traditions: lighting the Menorah, the story of the Christ child, bringing evergreen trees into our home, and pagan rituals of the rebirth of the Sun God from the womb of the Dark Mother.

The Sumerian tale of the descent of Inanna, Queen of Heaven and Earth, to the realm of Her sister Ereshkigal, Queen of the Underworld, takes us to the deepest roots of the mysteries of darkness and light, and death and rebirth.

Long ago, Inanna turned Her mind to the Great Below and chose to travel its precarious ways in search of Her greater becoming. At each of the gates to the Underworld, She removed a piece of Her royal vestments, until She stood, naked and humbled, before the throne of the mighty Ereshkigal. Inanna surrendered Herself to Ereshkigal in the belly of the dark. Death was the price of this journey and rebirth into Her true beauty and power was its gift.

Light must give over to dark to birth new light. Death is the gateway to rebirth. Our life story, with its trials and wounding, is the crucible of our greater becoming and deepest beauty.

Inanna knew these things; only through the ways of Ereshkigal and the Great Below could She rise up into Her full Goddess powers.

At the Winter Solstice, with Ereshkigal's powers palpable in the long, cold exhalation of the darkest night, the Great Below beckons. Your journey of soul asks you to follow Inanna's lead, and to brave the ways and mysteries of Ereshkigal and the sacred dark. To reclaim the powers and gifts of your Deep Self and authentic humanity, you must seek out the seeds of your beauty and wounding that are ready to return to the light of your conscious engagement. From these seeds, a new beginning of healing and personal growth is born.

The seasons of Nature turn. The dark gives way to the light, and the old to the new. Nothing lasts forever, nor is carved in stone. In these primal truths, you can find the hope and courage to change your life and our world for the better, birthing new light and beautiful possibilities from the darkest night of your wounding and the pain and sorrow of our collective humanity.

A Sabbat Mystery
Ereshkigal and Our Beauty and Wounding

On the longest night of the year, in the thick of the mysteries of the sacred dark, turn your mind to the Great Below and the fearsome voice of Ereshkigal:

"I am the still, held breath of the dark that precedes the dawn. I am the hands of the Earth that cup the seeds of new life. I am the dark powers that pulse within the fleshy matter of your body. I am the death that promises rebirth, and the kiss that awakens you from your death slumber. I am the keeper of the lost parts of your soul, and of secrets that can set you free."

Inanna turned Her mind to the Great Below and Her Goddess sister Ereshkigal. She surrendered everything, even Her life, to the Underworld mysteries of death and rebirth. And through these mysteries, Inanna was transformed into Her full Goddess presence and power.

As terrifying as this journey may seem, know that its rewards are immeasurable. On this darkest of nights, the seeds of brilliant new beginnings, within and without, are stirring from their death sleep, ready to return from the darkness to the light.

Be brave, follow in Inanna's footsteps. Make this conscious descent, stripping yourself bare of your worldly masks and illusions, and habits of belief, thought and action that stand between you and your truest, most beautiful potential. Do these things and Ereshkigal will grant you entry to Her realm and help you discover the seeds of your new beginning and the soul-based life you long for.

Ereshkigal does not rise from Her throne as you enter Her inner sanctum. She is dressed in a red velvet sheath that molds itself to Her voluptuous, curvy form, with a silver circlet as a crown and silver snake bangles on Her ankles and wrists. A smoky heat and feral power rises from Her amber skin and strong, bare limbs, marking Her as a dangerous, commanding being that could easily reduce you to ashes. With an imperial scrutiny, She pierces through your outer veneer into the core of your being. There is no hiding in Ereshkigal's realm.

Hold your own under Ereshkigal's probing, black-eyed stare, and stay in your center and power. As formidable as She appears, Ereshkigal's intention is to help you, not harm you, though She will ask much of you in service of your greater becoming.

"I know why you are here," Ereshkigal says, "You have dared to stand before my throne in the Great Below because you seek the miracle of my rebirth magic in your own life and journey of soul, where new beginnings emerge from death and darkness. But be warned, there is a price to be paid for so potent a magic. As the new dawn is born from the darkest night, so too the beautiful new beginnings you desire emerge from the depths of your wounding.

"Long has been the dark night of soul of your human species. Long have you done great harm to each other and to the good green Earth. Long have you run from the pain and sorrow of this grievous wound. Whatever personal wounding you carry is a reflection of this greater harm.

"But all is not gloom. Nothing lasts forever. The dark night of soul for you and your human kin is ending. A new dawn beckons for those brave enough to dare the rebirth magic of my Underworld realm. As a reward for your bravery, I will show you what you seek."

Ereshkigal leaves Her throne and circles around you. Her movements are sinuous and creature-like, and Her nostrils flare as She sniffs the air, seeming to take your measure from the scent-signature emanating from your form.

"However you have learned to deny and hide from your

wounding will not serve you in your pathwork with me," Ereshkigal whispers in your ear, "I strip you of these things so you can see the truth that is your life and your world, although you travel my ways by your own free will, and I never ask more than you are able to bear."

She presses Her hands, firm and hot, into the front and back of your mid-torso. Your mind and body become still, silent, empty. Whatever you think you know, think you are, think you want, vanish. There is only the pulsing, fleshy darkness of your inner landscape and the pulsing, potent darkness of Ereshkigal outside and inside of you.

"Where you find your wounding, you also find your beauty," She says, "When you show up to your pain, you also remember your joy. In stepping into the fullness of your life story, you shed a smallness of being for a bigness of presence and power."

As Ereshkigal withdraws Her hands, something passes through your skin. She uncurls Her fingers and two shining seeds rest within Her open palms.

"These are the seeds of your beauty and wounding that are waking within you," She says, "Within their compressed interior are the makings of a bright new beginning — a magic that can heal your soul, brewed from the potent meeting of your beauty and wounding. You cannot reclaim one without the other."

Ereshkigal turns your hands palm upward and places the warm, pulsing seeds within their cupped interior.

"These seeds come with challenge and choice," She says, "You can take them inside of you and then change will come. Or you can cast them back into the dark, but to no avail, because change will still come. What is waking in you will not let you rest until you have taken the next step closer to the soul-based life you are meant to live, and the new dawn waiting to be born from your inner darkness into the sunlit world."

The darkness around you begins to lighten as the longest night gives way to the returning light. Ereshkigal and Her realm grow fainter and fainter until they disappear altogether. Yet the power of Her presence and words remain, beckoning to you from the shining seeds.

One more time, be brave. Raise your hands to your lips and swallow the magic of these seeds whole. Take them inside of you and feel the stirrings of a new dawn within your gestating interior. Though you cannot know where these seeds will lead you in the months to come, you have dared the Great Below and claimed its powerful rebirth magic as your own. You have taken the next step into the soulful life that is yours to live in the weaving of a new-made world.

A Sabbat Teaching
Beauty In the Belly of the Dark

Nature settles ever deeper into Her cloak of darkness and repose at the Winter Solstice. At the opposite end of the scale, our Western culture marks the holiday season in a flurry of shopping, social obligations and overconsumption — a busy end to a busy year in an outward-focused, ever-doing, hungry-for-more world.

Nature remembers what we humans have forgotten: every cycle must return to stillness, silence, the dark; every out-breath requires an in-breath; every outer endeavor turns back inward to its origins, its center, and begins again; from death comes new life, and from the darkest night, the new dawn is born.

Beauty sleeps in the belly of the dark, be it the seeds of the green growth of Spring, the powers and mysteries of the unknown, and our own dormant gifts and potential. Yet the dark has a gatekeeper; the wounding of our pain, losses and the denied, repressed parts of our life story and humanity also await us in the belly of the dark. We cannot reclaim our beauty without also embracing and healing our wounding. Both dwell within the shadowed folds of our inner world, side by side, a mirror of the other, each with gifts and blessings to share.

The part of you that holds your wounding is not your nemesis; it is the truth keeper of how you were hurt, what was taken from you, and the choices you made to survive and even thrive in the face of adversity. It has stood guard and shielded your tender, beautiful Deep Self, waiting for the ripe moment of your healing and blossoming.

If you are one of the fortunate, with few bumps and bruises in your life story, still the darkness has gifts lying in wait for you. The sacred dark is the guardian of the vast potential of our authentic humanity that has been denied and repressed in our collective culture.

Open to the ways of Nature at this turning of the Winter Solstice. Heed the call arising from the belly of the dark that invites you to stillness, silence and the deepest mysteries of your inner world. Let go of the frenetic activities of the season; follow your breath inward and return to your center in search of the parts of your life story and Deep Self ready to step out of the shadowed folds of your psyche and into the light of your everyday life.

So without, so within. As the new dawn is born from the darkest night, so too your beauty blossoms from the depths of your wounding into the returning light of a newborn day.

Guided Meditation
Brave the Great Below

On the Winter Solstice eve, set up a cozy, private spot in your home where you can be warm and comfortable. Turn off the lights and have a candle close at hand, but do not light it. Close your eyes and begin to track the movements and sounds of your body with breath. On every in-breath, infuse yourself with the still, quiet darkness that surrounds you. On every out-breath, release any stress you may be carrying from the holiday season. Soften your facial muscles, loosen the stiff, tight places in your body, and empty your mind of thoughts and concerns. Be with yourself in the all-encompassing dark.

Open yourself to the natural world energies of this longest night of the year and the awakening tendrils of new light and new beginnings that will soon be birthed from this deep darkness. Imagine taking these energies into your body and sense them calling forth your inner darkness and emerging light. Let your soul longings bubble up to the surface, stirring up the seeds of new beginnings waiting for you in the belly of the dark.

Stay in your center and observe any emotional reactions that you may have. No matter what arises, be it fear, anticipation, pain or joy, just keep your breath slow and steady, and your body and awareness open and receptive. Winter Solstice work can be edgy, awakening painful, fragile places in your psyche. You travel these pathways by your free will, so set the intention to be guided by your highest good and only go as deep as is right for you at this moment.

Continue to breathe and ground, slow and steady; let go of your emotions and settle into the empty silence within you.

Like Inanna, turn your mind to the Great Below, seeking out its rebirth magic to guide your journey of soul. See a portal before you with a passageway that leads down, down, down to the realm of Ereshkigal, Queen of the Underworld. As you make your descent toward Ereshkigal's throne room, sense yourself traversing a series of gates where invisible hands strip you of your worldly masks and pretenses, and anything else that stands between you and the new beginning awaiting you this Winter Solstice eve.

At each of these gates, notice what is being taken from you, and how it feels to be free from its influence. Know that the ways you have learned to deny and hide from the truth that is your life, both the beautiful and painful, will only block your pathwork with Ereshkigal. But you engage this pathwork at your own pace, and need only strip yourself as bare as feels comfortable.

When you reach this point, you will find yourself on the threshold of Ereshkigal's throne room. Look deep, deep inside: is there one more thing that you are still clinging to that must be surrendered to the dark? Name this thing and gently let it fall away.

Step past the threshold and stand before Ereshkigal, empty and humble. Take in your surroundings: the look and feel of the Great Below, the fearsome and beautiful presence of Ereshkigal on Her throne, and your physical, emotional and energetic responses to this sacred, powerful place.

Bear Ereshkigal's scrutiny in silence, waiting for Her to speak and direct your engagement. This is Her sovereign realm, and you are here by Her grace and consent. Yet also stand proud and sure of yourself; you have made this descent and brave this encounter of your own volition.

There is no hiding in Ereshkigal's presence. She knows why you are here and what you seek in the deepest dark of this Winter Solstice eve. Speak words of respect, and humbly request that She help you activate Her rebirth magic and discover the seeds of your beauty and wounding waking within you.

Ereshkigal descends from Her throne and directs your attention to a mirror of polished, black stone. This mirror has special powers; it can reveal the parts of your inner landscape and life story that are ready to return from the shadow places in your psyche to the light of your conscious awareness.

Focus your awareness on its reflective surface, and whisper to the mirror, "show me my beauty and wounding."

Open yourself to the images and energies the mirror reveals: the hidden gifts, dormant potential and secret desires of your beauty, along with the repressed and forgotten pain, losses and suffering of your wounding. Do not deny or push anything away. But do practice self-care, and only delve as deep into your wounding as feels right for you.

Remember that your wounding is your ally, not your nemesis, and that the dark holds the lost jewels of your Deep Self and authentic humanity that have long waited to return to their rightful place and purpose in your waking life. You cannot move forward in reclaiming your beauty without also reclaiming your mirror wounding.

See the intertwining of your beauty and wounding, and the blessings and challenges offered by each. Spend as much time as you need to connect with these vital roots of your life story and spiritual unfolding. Then reach for the parts of your beauty and wounding that are meant to guide your journey of soul at this time, and imagine them transforming into warm, fleshy seeds in your cupped palms. From these seeds, your pathwork of new beginnings will be born.

Hold the seeds outward for Ereshkigal's perusal. Like Inanna, surrender yourself to Ereshkigal's wisdom and ways. Heed Her words of guidance on the potent pathwork offered by these seeds, and let Her presence and rebirth magic settle into your flesh and bones. Though She can be a fierce and demanding taskmistress, Ereshkigal's sacred intention is to help you transform into the fullness of your Deep Self.

If you are ready to do the pathwork revealed to you this Winter Solstice eve, bring these seeds of beauty and wounding to your lips and swallow them as a conscious act of receiving and ingesting their transformative energies. And in this powerful act, know that you have truly begun the work of mending and reclaiming your beauty and wounding, and of birthing a bright new beginning on your journey of soul.

Look one last time into Ereshkigal's eyes as you bid Her farewell, seeing beyond Her ferocity to Her infinite love. Bow and offer Her your gratitude and reverence, for it is She who has guarded these lost parts of your life story and Deep Self, and the rebirth mysteries of the sacred dark, for the time when you would remember Her sacred presence and your own.

Use your breath to bring yourself back to waking consciousness and your physical body. Open your eyes and sit for a few minutes in the enveloping darkness. Then light a candle as a symbol of the new light and new beginning that will be born of this Winter Solstice magic with Ereshkigal. Take this light into your core, infusing the seeds in your belly with the hope and promise that from death comes new life, and from the darkest night of your wounding, the new dawn of your beauty is born.

Inner Pathwork
The Wounded Parts of Your Life Story

None of us are immune to the destructive ways and the

oppressive history of humanity. We are born, raised, indoctrinated and exposed to hurtful, abusive experiences within the toxicity of status quo reality. Our personal and ancestral stories are weighed down with an accumulation of negative, painful memories and energies that hold our loss, grief and dysfunction. We deny, repress and pave over these wounded parts of our life story, burying them within the shadowy folds of our psyche.

When we do descent pathwork, we open to our inner darkness and shadow, and expose ourselves to the repressed parts of our wounding. This can go against the grain of our survival instincts and culture-based impulses to make the hurt, dysfunctional places inside of us the enemy, and to run as fast as we can in the other direction. Yet to do so is to prolong our suffering and block our healing.

The sacred feminine offers an alternative, positive frame that transforms our wounding from our nemesis to a sacred, cherished partner on our journey of soul. With this frame, our wounded parts keep the truth of how we were hurt, guard the jewels of our Deep Self and true beauty, and remember the secret stories that can set us free.

Try on this sacred feminine frame of embracing your wounding as your cherished partner, and see how it changes your relationship with the painful places inside of you. Whenever you engage your personal wounding, it is essential that you move slowly and gently. Remember to draw upon your ethos of radical self-care from the Fall Equinox pathwork, and your magic cup of the good from Samhain. Always make sure you have a good support system and professional assistance if needed, before you delve too deeply into your wounded places.

Set the intention to only do the pathwork that you are ready to engage.

Start by opening your heart to your wounded parts as if they are long, lost friends or hurt, orphaned children in need of kindness and support. If a friend or a child was suffering, you would not deny their pain, vilify them and turn your back on their stories, so give yourself the same compassion and tender attention.

See if one particular aspect of your wounding rises into your awareness, perhaps linked to the seeds that came to you in your Winter Solstice meditation. Open yourself to this connection and any information and energy that come through, such as: body sensations, intense emotion, a vague remembrance, a detailed memory or a younger part of yourself that had a hurtful experience.

Imagine this initial encounter as the tip of the iceberg, with hidden depth beneath the surface, or as a first date, knowing that, like any relationship, it will take time to get to know and trust each other.

Welcome whatever shows up and start a conversation. A great way to have this conversation is through journaling or by using your preferred form of creative expression. Take a few deep breaths; let go of any judgment or preconception; be present in your love and desire to know more; and then let this wounded part of you speak on the empty page. Again, this communication can take on many forms: words, images, insights, body sensations and emotions. If things feel awkward and uncomfortable, just do your best and stay with your love.

When this communion feels complete, express your gratitude and promise to continue your conversation at another time. Then use your breath to center in your core, and check in with yourself. How did this encounter feel? What did you learn about your wounding? What did you learn about your beauty? How are your beauty and wounding linked in this part of your life story? How do these insights help you better understand your journey of soul at this time, and the seeds of your beauty and wounding that came to you in your Winter Solstice meditation? Has your attitude toward your personal wounding shifted? How can you continue and deepen the conversation you have started? Though you may not have answers to some of these questions, trust that the answers are there, just waiting to be revealed in your next communication and those that follow.

A positive, substantive relationship with the wounded parts of your life story is essential to your Path of She work. Ereshki-gal's Winter Solstice wisdom teaches us that we cannot recover our beauty without our wounding, and together they weave the magic that can heal our soul and our collective humanity. With this first encounter, you have begun a new relationship with your personal wounding. Continue to deepen this communion, finding your own forms of communication and partnership. With time and trust, your wounded parts will offer up their precious gifts of truth and secrets that just might set you free.

Outer Pathwork
Inner Stillness in the Outer World

At no time of the year is the contrast between the ways of Nature and the ways of humanity more apparent than at the Winter Solstice. While the wild realm marks the end of the solar cycle by turning inward to its deepest darkness and stillness, our Western culture brings the year-end to a holiday-festivity crescendo of overconsumption and overstimulation.

Nature remembers what we humans have forgotten: every cycle must return to stillness, silence, and every out-breath requires an in-breath. Can we learn to emulate Nature by cultivating an inner stillness and silence while still engaging the outer world? The answer is yes, and though this skill doesn't come easy, it's as close as our next breath.

To learn this skill, you must first master breath meditation. In its basic form, breath meditation is the practice of emptying your mind and focusing your awareness on the movements, sounds and sensations of your breath. Slow, soft, rhythmic — in through the nose, out through the nose — belly rounding outward on the inhalation, and compressing inward on the exhalation. If your mind wanders or becomes noisy, as soon as you notice return your focused attention to your breath. Practice this base skill until you can still your mind and cultivate inner silence for extended intervals — first five, then ten, then twenty minutes and longer, building your mastery of this simple yet very powerful skill.

Then modify this exercise to use your breath to anchor in your Deep Self. Focus your awareness on your solar plexus while also tracking the movements, sounds and sensations of your breath. You can place your hands on your mid-body to help anchor your concentration in your core. As you track your breath, imagine on every inhalation that you are sinking deeper and deeper into your inner landscape and the knowing of your Deep Self. When it feels right, let go of your focus on your breath, and open yourself to whatever sensations, insights and information come to you from the depths of your inner landscape. Again, this is a simple but powerful skill that helps you to step aside of your outward-focused, thinking-mind engagement of the world, and to source instead from the wellspring of your Deep Self.

Once you have mastered this skill, you are ready to try it out in your waking life. Pick a touchstone activity, something you do several times every day, like making a cup of tea. When you do this activity, check in with your breath, focus on the inhalation and let it anchor you in your Deep Self. Then feel how this shifts your center of awareness and your relationship to the outer world.

Now try this activity when you get up in the morning, before you go to sleep at night, and at key transitions in your day, such as when you first arrive at work. Again, use your breath to anchor in your Deep Self and inner landscape, and then check in with your external environment. Keep practicing this skill until you get so good that you can use it anytime you need it. With just a few deep, conscious breaths, you can be present in an external situation centered in the power and clarity of your Deep Self.

Though it may take you many seasons to master the skill of engaging the outer world from your inner stillness and depth, the Winter Solstice can be your inspiration and reminder that every outer endeavor turns back inward to its origins, its center, and begins again. You too can turn your awareness inward, to your center and the wellspring of your Deep Self, and begin again. This wondrous, powerful ability is always just a breath away.

Walk the Path
The Yes of New Year's Resolutions

The turning of the calendar year closely follows the beginning of a new solar cycle at the Winter Solstice. Traditionally this is a time to make New Year's resolutions.

On the Path of She, we work with yes magic. Yes is the most

powerful magical word in our vocabulary. It is the word that the Universe pays closest attention to. Say 'yes' and doors of possibilities open. Say 'yes' from the depths of soul, and we can transform our life.

Yes magic aligns the dynamo powers of desire (what we want) and will (our ability to make things happen) through a specific, consciously chosen intention. When we make a New Year's resolution, we are focusing our will by setting our intention for the coming calendar year. This is a perfect opportunity to use yes magic in service of our journey of soul.

To make a New Year's resolution in alignment with your journey of soul, you need to start with your desire. The core desire that drives Path of She work is healing and reclaiming your Deep Self and authentic humanity. In your Winter Solstice meditation, this core desire infused your pathwork in Ereshkigal's realm, and led you to the seeds of your beauty and wounding that will guide your journey of soul in the weeks and months to come.

In setting your New Year's resolution, tune into these seeds gestating inside of you and the insights you gained in your meditation encounter with Ereshkigal. What healing and personal changes do the seeds suggest? What are your fears and hopes? What new skills, knowledge, lifestyle enhancements and resources would support your pathwork process and ensure self-care?

Remember that these seeds are newly emerged from the darkness to the light of your conscious awareness and engagement. This is the beginning of your communion and relationship with the stories, secrets and gifts they have to offer you. An ideal New Year's resolution would support and nurture the new direction of your spiritual journey, without being overly directive or goal-oriented. For example, you could set a resolution to develop a new skill, knowledge area or lifestyle choice that would support and enhance your emerging pathwork.

In the coming weeks, follow through on your resolution, backing your yes words with yes actions. In addition, continue to explore the seeds of your beauty and wounding. You have activated these powerful energies in your meditation, and now they will start to reveal themselves in the insights, dreams, issues, challenges and opportunities that come your way. Expect to be surprised, to dig into places that you would rather avoid, and to be led by mysteries that you don't fully understand.

With your inner pathwork exercise, you have begun to cultivate a deeper relationship with your personal wounding.

Continue this essential pathwork, healing and strengthening your communion and communication with the wounded parts of your story and psyche. This is tender, sensitive work, so proceed at a pace that is right for you, ensuring you have the necessary personal and professional resources and support to ensure your self-care.

Also practice your outer pathwork activities to develop your skills of breath meditation, centering in your Deep Self, and engaging the outer world from your inner stillness and depth. These are powerful skills that bring presence and clarity to your Path of She work, and the demands of your everyday life.

Even though the new solar year has begun, darkness still holds sway in the natural realm. You too are still traveling the dark ways of the sacred feminine, beyond the edge of your known world into the wondrous new beginnings that await you.

IMBOLC

Winter gives way
to Spring at Imbolc.
Light and shadow dance together
as you tend the seeds
of your beauty and wounding
that will heal and transform
your life.

A t Imbolc, dormant hungers are stirring on your journey of soul. As the seasons turn from Winter into Spring, the returning powers of light and life activate your longing for new beginnings, and coax you to leave behind the stasis of what you know to seek out new possibilities.

The Earth is waking at Imbolc, casting off Her winter cloak of cold and darkness, and prodding the natural realm to stir from its long rest at the first signs of Spring. Nothing seems certain at this time of year. Nature can be in the throes of snow and frigid temperatures, or it can offer up warm, sunny days that entice brave snowdrops to rise from the still-frozen soil. No matter how hard Winter tries to hang on, the days get steadily longer and warmer, and Nature opens itself once more to the life-giving powers of the strengthening sun.

Groundhog Day is the secular custom that coincides with Imbolc. The groundhog is a weather diviner; according to tradition, if the groundhog emerges from its hole and sees its shadow then Winter will be digging in for another six weeks. If it doesn't see its shadow, Spring is near at hand. Regardless of the groundhog's prediction, Imbolc is a time when we turn our mind and intentions toward the seeds we would like to plant in the Spring, both in our garden and in our life.

Like the natural realm, what has been dormant within you hungers for new growth. And like the groundhog, light and shadow are both part of your dance with the shifting, seasonal energies.

At Imbolc, you turn your mind to the seeds that hold the next pieces of your pathwork, sourced from the beauty and wounding of your Deep Self and life story. As you draw these seeds into the light of your conscious awareness and engagement, you will also encounter the shadow-side of the wounded, denied parts of your life and our world.

To journey on the Path of She is to accept and work with your whole/holy nature and life story, both the light and shadow, and beauty and wounding. You cannot truly change yourself or your outer world without showing up to the naked, raw truth of who you are and what you've experienced. Self-awareness, self-acceptance and compassion are essential components of the hard work of healing and transforming your life.

You need not be alone in this momentous task. Brigid is a mighty Goddess, with powers of healing and inspiration, who comes to us through Celtic mythology. Some tales of Brigid tell how She came to the Earth when all was blackness and chaos, and placed Her mantle around the planet, transforming it into a place of beauty. Brigid has endured through the turning times of humanity, both as Goddess and as Saint, and Imbolc is Her festival day.

Brigid draws us to Her doorstep at Imbolc. She has so many gifts to offer us: the light of Her sacred flame to lead us out of the darkness; the healing, inspirational waters of Her holy well to mend our hurts and guide our journey; and the transformational powers of Her forge where the old can be recast into the new.

These wondrous things Brigid will grant you, but you must seek Her out in Her realm between the worlds, and consciously choose to embrace Her healing ways. And you must make a vow, a soul commitment, to tend the seeds of your beauty and wounding, and to follow where they lead you on your journey of soul. She can offer you healing, wisdom and support, but only you can do the hard work of transforming your life and mending our world.

A Sabbat Mystery
Brigid and the Making of Vows

In the velvet darkness between the worlds, a welcoming light shines bright and steady. Here Brigid tends Her holy well and sacred flame, offering up their life-transforming magic that grants the gifts of healing, inspiration and wisdom for those who seek Her guidance. She does not call us to Her side, for She knows that we will find Her when the time is ripe.

As Nature shifts from the dark dormancy of Winter to the life-inducing powers of the strengthening sun that herald the approach of Spring, our desire for the spring of new possibilities and the end of the long winter of our soul drives us to Brigid's doorstep. Our mind turns to the seeds of our beauty and wounding, sourced from our Deep Self and life story, that hold the next pieces of our pathwork. And our soul turns to Brigid's loving, gracious presence and Her tremendous powers that can make our life anew.

Trust these powerful hungers and impulses stirring within you. Trust that life-transforming change is possible, and that Brigid can help you in this essential soul work. Trust that your shining inner light is kin to Her shining light, and in the spirit of this kinship, you will find your way to Her realm between the worlds.

When you reach the threshold of Brigid's realm, you'll discover a thick oak door with an ancient key, greened by age and the elements – the key of conscious choice. Your soul desire has led you to Brigid, now you must consciously choose to turn the key, knowing that to stand before this mighty, generous Goddess is to commit yourself to Her healing ways. And once you have made this commitment, it is not easily unmade; when you open the door that connects you to Brigid, it can never truly be shut again.

As you step over the threshold, Brigid welcomes you with a warm, captivating smile, Her cheeks flushed slightly with the heat of Her forge. She is breathtaking to behold, with long, fiery-red tresses, creamy-white skin, and a tall, slender form draped in a dark-green mantle. Though Her beauty is as bright as the flames She tends, it is the palpable presence of Her love and kindness that is your strongest impression of Her.

Both the flames and Brigid's radiance seep through your flesh, swiftly thawing the frozen places in your heart. When you look into Her startling-green eyes, you see the life you are longing for reflected in their soulful depths, and Her desire to help make your dreams come true. You do not need to speak these things to Brigid, She already knows you, inside and out, deep and true.

"Let us see what hidden knowledge and healing visions await you at this time of Imbolc," She says.

With Her long, expressive fingers, Brigid beckons you to a shallow, black stone bowl filled with the waters of Her holy well. She directs your gaze to its still, flat surface, illuminated by the flickering lights of Her sacred flame.

Images arise in a swift procession from the close up and intimate of your life to the wide scope of the greater world. Brigid's scrying waters do not spare you from the ugly and the painful. You are shown the hurt places inside of you and their symbiotic expression in your outer existence, and then, broader still, to the same patterns that exist in human society.

"These images tell the one story of the seed of your wounding," Brigid says, "What is inside is outside, and what is outside is inside; your inner world reveals itself in your outer existence, and your personal life is both trapped within the strictures of collective reality and you help re-create this reality with your day-to-day choices and actions."

Brigid passes Her hands over the basin's surface and new images appear, this time offering a melange of the beautiful and inspiring, again drawing both on your personal life and the greater world. Some of the images you recognize from your current existence and others feel achingly familiar, like a longed-for possibility that has yet to take form.

"These images tell the one story of the seed of your beauty," Brigid says, "Just as with your wounding, what is inside and outside both inform and infuse the other. By the beauty and goodness of individuals, the beauty and goodness of human society emerges."

With a swirling motion of her fingertips, Brigid activates Her holy water's visionary magic one last time. The previous images blend and merge, entwining the stories of your beauty and wounding, both in their personal and collective manifestations. And you see, from the depths of your being, that your beauty and wounding are mirrors of the same thing. There is really only one story, the story of your life, woven from all that you are, and all that you've ever experienced, defined and constrained within the matrix of collective reality.

Together you step away from the scrying bowl. Brigid turns to face you and says, "Everything has a place and purpose, even the most painful and challenging of these images. Life, with its joys and sorrows, is the crucible of your spiritual healing and evolution. You would not be who you are now, standing here with me on the cusp of your greater becoming, without having gone through these trials and experiences. Great beauty and power are forged from great wounding and suffering, tempered by a wisdom, love and compassion that a life fully embraced, in its light and shadow, can grant you.

"My scrying bowl has revealed to you the seeds and stories that are the makings of the new beginning ready to emerge from within you. They are the raw materials that will drive the healing pathwork that is before you now.

"You must tend these seeds in preparation for your springtime of new growth. Your life is their soil, your love their water, and your conscious awareness their sunshine. With proper care, they will show you the way of your healing and transformation, and your path forward to the life of soul you are longing for."

"Are you ready to take this next crucial step on your journey of soul? Will you commit yourself to the sacred task of tending your seeds of beauty and wounding, and letting them guide you in your pathwork?"

Think hard before you answer Brigid, for this is a special, powerful kind of commitment — a vow spoken before Her sacred forge, where the old is made anew. She will hold you to this commitment, and your life will be forever changed.

With a simple "yes", you bind yourself to Brigid.

"So it is chosen, so it will be," She says.

Three times Her hammer strikes Her anvil, hard steel against hard steel, ringing your vow outward into the listening Universe.

Then Brigid kisses your brow and presses Her palm against your solar plexus. A warm, swirling energy passes between you, and you sense the visions of Her scrying waters now alive and brewing in your belly center. She smiles one last smile, filling the space and your heart with Her radiance, and then She is gone.

Yet Her kiss remains, a token that She will never leave your side. The visioning magic of this Imbolc will bring you the healing, inspiration and wisdom you need to tend your seeds of beauty and wounding. As you tend your seeds, discovering and embracing their place and purpose on your journey of soul, Brigid tends them with you, coaxing out their healing and creative impulses. And as you shift and grow, bringing positive change to your life and the greater world, Her joy shines down on you, filling you up with the bright flame of Her nourishing love.

A Sabbat Teaching
The Shadow Dance

At Imbolc, Winter is waning and the season turns toward Spring. The groundhog is said to be a predictor of the arrival of springtime. If the groundhog sees its shadow, off it goes back into its hole, informing us that Winter won't be letting go soon. If it doesn't see its shadow, Spring is on its way.

This shadow dance is familiar to us humans. As the shifting light and warming days coax the groundhog from its den in search of the quickening signs of Spring, so does our hunger for the spring of new beginnings coax us to leave behind the refuge of what we know and sniff the air for signs of shifting possibilities. What we seek draws us into the light of greater consciousness, and where there is light there is shadow.

Shadow in our human psyche is the depository of the repressed, denied and vilified parts of our personal lives and human society: our pain, dysfunction and unpalatable, uncontrollable instincts and emotions. When we encounter our personal or collective shadow, our first impulse, like the groundhog, is to retreat into the blinders and comforts of our old ways and their winter-like grip of stagnation and stasis.

What we forget in this retreat impulse is that light and shadow dance together. There

*cannot be one without the other. We humans
are woven of light and shadow, of good and
bad qualities and instincts, and of things
known and mysteries yet to be discovered.*

We forget, in our fear and projections, that the shadow
realm also holds the raw materials of our deeper potential.
And that the things we repress, deny and vilify just might be
exactly what we need — secret truths, hidden gifts and latent
powers — to heal, grow and flourish.

In our forgetting, we act out from our repressed and denied
places, and doom ourselves and our world to be ruled by
that which we refuse to face and claim as part of our human
experience.

In our forgetting, we become half-human, shut off from
essential parts of our nature and selfhood, and truncated in our
self-knowing, expression and evolution.

Imbolc is a between time, of Winter thawing into Spring,
and of the dark giving way to the light. We are not separate
from these natural energies and their life-seeking drives.
Nor can we leave our shadow behind as we reach out to the
springtime call of new possibilities, personal growth and
societal change. Rather than giving into our instinct to retreat
from our shadow, transformative change comes when we have
the courage and compassion to reach out our hand and heart
to our shadow, and to step together into the returning powers
of light and life.

Guided Meditation
Light and Shadow of Soul Work

On the eve of Imbolc, light a candle in a private corner of
your home. Bring your face close and let its flame dance its

teasing warmth across your skin. Track your breath, slow, slow in and slow, slow out, relaxing ever deeper into the physical movements of your body with breath. Imagine your inner light and heat becoming stronger with every breath, just as the sun is becoming stronger with every day. Let this inner heat thaw the frozen-over places inside of you that hold your stagnation and resistance to change and new growth.

When you feel present and centered in your body, focus on the candle's golden light; use its shimmering energies to shift your awareness to the place between the worlds where Brigid's sacred flame burns brilliant and strong. Put your hands on your belly and sense the heat of Her fire infusing the seeds of your beauty and wounding that are stirring at this turning time, calling you to new growth and possibilities. Let these potent forces draw you to Her doorstep.

Now close your eyes and imagine yourself at the threshold of Brigid's realm. There is a thick door in front of you, with a smooth-worn handle and a key poised within its lock. Place one hand on the handle and the other on the key. Take a few breaths to anchor once more in your center and to bring your complete attention to this moment.

Feel your hunger to shift your life in new, positive directions. Feel any pain or resistance that this hunger may trigger. Know that when you open this door and cross its threshold to stand before Brigid, you are choosing to heal and grow, bringing these light and shadow energies with you.

Make your next movements deliberate and conscious, a shifting from the winter-like stagnation of what you know into the spring-filled possibilities of what can be. Then turn the key, step through the door and find yourself fully present in Brigid's sacred realm.

Imagine Brigid welcoming you with open arms. Take in the details of Her radiant beauty and the powerful energies of Her holy well and sacred flame. Orient yourself within Her realm and its potent magic that can make your life anew. Ask Brigid to share with you Her gifts of inspiration and wisdom, and to help you better understand the seeds of your beauty and wounding that are driving your pathwork at this time.

Brigid leads you to Her scrying bowl, filled with the waters of Her holy well and lit by Her sacred flame. Merge with the flickering dance of flames across the flat, still surface of the water. Open your inner landscape to these heady powers, knowing that they can reveal the hidden knowledge within you and share healing visions of where your journey of soul will lead you next.

As Brigid's holy waters divulge these secrets and visions, enter deeply into the stories woven into the seeds of your beauty and wounding. Information and insights can come to you in many ways: through visual imagery, a voice that speaks to you, or body sensations and energies. Fully engage whatever shows up, in whatever form. Take your time, ask questions, dive deep.

Decipher how these seeds manifest in your everyday life and the wide world around you, and how they inform your journey of soul. Seek out the parts of your Deep Self and life story that are calling for healing and reclaiming. Gather what insights you can on how to best tend these seeds and follow their lead in your emerging pathwork of new beginnings.

Notice on the wall behind you that your shadow shimmies and shifts in sync with the flames of Brigid's forge. Light and shadow are partners in your soul work. What you have lost, your shadow remembers; what is most precious within you, your shadow protects; what you need to tend and heal, your shadow will bring to your attention. You cannot reclaim your beauty without your wounding, nor your joy without your pain.

Widen your heart to your shadow-side, accepting that everything you are and everything you have experienced, the good and the bad, the joyful and the painful, have brought you to this moment and serve as the raw materials of your greater becoming. Then turn your awareness back to Brigid's scrying bowl. Ask it to reveal anything else you need to know at this time, including your imperfections, limitations and resistance that are the shadow reflections of your hunger for new beginnings. These too are essential pieces of your journey of soul.

When your scrying magic feels complete, step back from its potent energies and turn to face Brigid. You have a choice to make before you leave Her presence; you must decide, given all that you have been shown this Imbolc eve, whether you are ready to tend these stirring seeds within you, with your shadow-side as partner and ally.

Know that your yes is a vow that goes both ways; your pledge is to do the hard work of reclaiming a life of soul, and Brigid's promise is to love and support you at every step on your way.

Speak your vow to Brigid; name the pathwork and new beginnings that you are ready to commit to in the coming Spring season. Feel the power of your vow amplified by the magic of Brigid's forge, where the old is made anew. And sense the greater powers and mysteries, beyond the walls of Brigid's realm, that heed your vow and align themselves in service of your greater becoming.

For a few more minutes, gaze into Brigid's eyes; drink in the details of Her exquisite features and fill yourself up with the love that permeates every ounce of Her being. Then bring your time with Brigid to a close. Listen to Her final words of guidance and wisdom. Share your gratitude and love, and bid Her farewell. Then use your breath to bring yourself back into your physical body and waking reality.

Open your eyes and take in the dance of shadow and candlelight in the room. Feel this mirror dance inside of you, and in the world around you. There is no light without shadow, good without bad, nor joy without pain. In the coming months, as you nurture and grow the new beginnings you have committed yourself to this Imbolc eve, remember this essential, inescapable truth: you are woven of all these things, and of mysteries unknown still sleeping in the shadow realm, waiting for their quickening moment to return to the light.

Inner Pathwork
Door to the Mysteries

In my late twenties, I had the enlightening experience of standing before William Hunt's life-sized painting of Christ, The Light of the World, in St. Paul's Cathedral in London. The image is of Christ standing before a closed door, with a lantern in one hand and preparing to knock with the other. There is no handle on the door; it can only be opened from the inside.

I was deeply moved by the painting and immediately understood its message (notwithstanding the Christian imagery) that my relationship with spirituality required an act of conscious choice on my part. When the Mysteries arrive on my doorstep, I must open the door and say yes to their guiding light before they can actively engage me in my pathwork.

In tales of the Goddess Brigid, She is a healer whose gifts of inspiration and wisdom can mend and evolve souls. These stories are not fantasies, but encoded teachings that, like the evocative painting of Christ, reveal our relationship to pow-erful, benevolent beings and energies that infuse and inform our waking-world reality. They tell us that these Mysteries can guide, inspire and fuel our spiritual evolution and journey toward wholeness.

When we say yes to the Mysteries, what we need, within and without, will show up in the right form and measure, in accordance with our soul-sourced needs. We are not alone, and never were.

The Imbolc mediation guides you to the threshold of Brigid's realm where you discover a door with a key. When you turn this key and open the door, you are consciously choosing to stand before Brigid and commit yourself to Her healing ways; you are saying yes to Brigid, granting Her permission to guide your pathwork. Later you are given the opportunity to make a vow to Brigid by naming and committing to the pathwork revealed in your meditation vision. Vow making is a more potent yes-commitment that solidifies the mutual bond between yourself and Brigid in support of your journey of soul.

In the language of the Path of She: when you say yes to the Mysteries, change will come. And that change will be what you need, not what you expect, and will likely include both the work of your beauty and your wounding. This change can reveal itself in many ways: through the symbol-rich content of your nighttime dreams, in synchronistic events in your waking life, by presenting you with wonderful opportunities and by landing you flat on your butt. No matter the form or content, whatever shows up is your pathwork of soul.

As part of preparing yourself to work with Brigid and other Mysteries, take some time to assess the state of the door that connects you to these beings and energies. Is your door slammed shut, open a crack or wide open? Is it neglected and overgrown with weeds and brambles, or have you consciously chosen and cultivated your relationship with the Mysteries? If you have worked with the Mysteries before, how have they come knocking on your door? Do you have a spiritual lens, belief system or process that frames and delineates your engagement of these powers, or is your approach more open-ended and experiential? Do they visit you in your dreams, through events and situations in your waking life, or through your spiritual practice? How do you commune with them: through words, sensations, images, intuitive leaps or some other form of communication and connection? If spirituality is new to you, how ready are you to open your door and consciously say yes to the Mysteries?

In asking yourself these questions, you are determining your state of openness toward Brigid and other Mysteries. If this is new to you, imagine opening the door a crack and seeing what happens. If you already have an established relationship and means of connecting with the Mysteries, see if you are limiting this process through your existing spiritual lens, beliefs or practices.

Most important, remember to stay anchored in your intention to heal and grow in alignment with your highest good when engaging any power or being outside of yourself, even the beautiful, caring Brigid. Just like in the human world, the Mysteries are inhabited by the good, the bad and the ugly. You only want to open your door to positive powers that serve and support your personal pathwork and spiritual evolution.

Outer Pathwork
Inner World, Outer Mirrors

Self-awareness of the light, shadow, beauty and wounding of

our inner landscape, outer existence and life story are essential to our journey of soul. This self-awareness gives rise to the focus and specifics that direct our pathwork. Yet it's not easy to see ourselves clearly, especially the parts, both beautiful and shadow, that we deny and push away.

The outer world can assist us in developing greater self-awareness by offering mirrors to our inner landscape.

Our inner world is infused and informed by the outer world; what is inside is outside, and what is outside is inside. The wonders of the natural realm and the loving presence of another person can help us sense and remember our true beauty. The unsavory aspects of our culture and negative behaviors of someone in our life can stir up the shadow of our personal story and traits.

This week expand your self-awareness of your inner beauty and shadow-side, deepening the insights you gained in your Imbolc mediation with Brigid. Remember to be gentle, compassionate and kind with yourself. Everyone has positive and not-so-positive qualities and experiences. Also, only take this exercise as far as you are ready to go at this time. When engaging the painful parts of your life story, make sure you have the support and resources you need to help you with your pathwork.

Start by focusing your awareness on the beauty in your environment, both from the natural and human realms. Spend time in your favorite wild space. Revel in the exquisite filigree of winter-bare branches, the stirring signs of life emerging from their seasonal sleep or whatever wild beauty speaks to your soul. Have lunch with one of your favorite people. Carefully observe the interactions of others that emanate positive energies. Know that the beauty that calls to you in the outer world is a direct mirror of the beauty that is inside of you. See what these wondrous experiences illuminate in your inner landscape, and what they teach you about your own positive qualities. Take these insights to heart and let them shift your self-image and awareness.

After you have juiced yourself up with beauty, turn your awareness to the shadow-side of your environment, focusing on things that you find repellent in the mainstream culture and in the people around you. Immerse yourself in the media and its endless, bad-news headlines. As you go about your daily life, notice attitudes, behaviors and issues that speak to the negative aspects of our human society. Consider someone in your life whose behavior is harmful or abusive to others. With each of these activities, pay close attention to your emotional reactions and any inner shadow that arises in you. This can include parts of your wounding story, someone who has hurt you or your own negative behaviors and traits. Remember to be gentle and compassionate with yourself and others. Again take in these insights and let them deepen your self-awareness.

At the end of the week, spend some time reflecting on what you've learned about yourself, and how these insights inform the pathwork that is emerging for you. What new things did you discover about your beauty, wounding and shadow-side in terms of your personal story, behaviors and traits? What spoke most deeply to your heart? How does this new information supplement and clarify the visions and insights that came to you in your Imbolc meditation? Specifically consider this question in relation to: the focus of your emerging pathwork; what you are being called to heal and reclaim; and how to best tend the seeds of your beauty and wounding that hold the next pieces of your pathwork.

Be patient with yourself as you engage these activities and

questions. Self-awareness is both a skill that takes time and practice to develop, and a resource that feeds and informs your journey of soul. You don't need perfect answers or perfect knowledge to embrace new beginnings. As part of the task of tending your seeds, you increase self-awareness of your beauty, wounding and shadow-side, and embrace the pathwork that comes to you from this greater self-awareness. There is only ever the work of this moment, and this work inextricably leads to the next step, and the one after that. Your self-awareness expands and deepens in tandem with this process.

Remember to stay in a place of self-acceptance and compassion for all that you are and all that you have experienced. When self-awareness is coupled with self-acceptance, you create an indomitable elixir of personal transformation, with love as the guiding light in the brave, hard work of reclaiming a life of soul.

Walk the Path
Your Life is Your Art

Perhaps John Lennon was channeling Brigid, in Her guise as the patroness of poets, when he said, "Our life is our art."

We were put on this good green Earth to make beauty, joy and love, no matter what life brings our way. Art is not something that belongs only to the creatives in our midst, but to every single one of us. We can be artists in our words, choices, deeds and creations. There are countless ways to bring goodness, joy, beauty, laughter and wisdom to our lives and the lives of others. And in doing so, we are making the art of life.

Keep this principle in mind in the weeks to come as you

continue to expand your self-awareness and self-acceptance, and to tend the seeds of your beauty and wounding, drawing on the insights and information you have gathered through your Imbolc mediation and outer pathwork. Hold the seeds up to the light of your conscious awareness, stand by your vow to Brigid to heal and grow, and change will come, in its own way and time, but it will come.

When this change is something unexpected, overwhelming, unpleasant or downright horrible, take a deep breath, find your center and highest-good intention, and then open the door that connects you to Brigid and the Mysteries that you explored in your inner pathwork exercise. Listen to their guidance, accept their support and know that whatever comes to you is your pathwork of soul. You are not, and never were, alone.

If you feel weighed down by your life's challenges, or if the wounding of your past threatens to drag everything under its shadowy tow, widen your eyes and heart and take a good look around you. Drink in the seasonal viewscape in your part of the world, which may be lingering in the grip of Winter or showing the early signs of Spring. No matter if the conditions are cold and dark, or warm and bright, Nature weaves art with the elements — in the swirling, sparkling dance of the last snowfall or the brave green shoots reaching skyward to embrace the strengthening sun.

Our world and your life are drenched in beauty. Art in the making is everywhere and in everything. This beauty is an alternative, balancing perspective that can shine light into your shadowy places, and offer a healing balm to your suffering and wounding. Great beauty is forged out of great wounding; the best of our human nature is often most apparent in the worst of situations — these powerful truths apply to your journey of soul.

This is your life. Grab hold of it. Change what weighs you down. Embrace what makes you shine. Gather close those things that make your soul sing. Look for the silver linings of personal growth in life's challenges. Cultivate resources and support to do your work deeply, wisely, safely. Do your very best and give your very best, no matter what comes your way. Celebrate your successes and honor your failures. Love yourself and remember to laugh in the messiness of it all.

Light, shadow, beauty, wounding, joy, pain — these are parts of your human experience, not to be escaped but to be embraced as the raw materials of your greater becoming. When you use these raw materials to heal and grow, from a place of self-awareness, self-acceptance and compassion, and from your profound longing to live a soul-based life, the new and beautiful will naturally arise from your pathwork. From these depths, you will make glorious, unforgettable art with your life, painted in the broad, brilliant strokes of your courage, goodness, wisdom and love.

Every journey unfolds from exactly where you are, and this place is always exactly where you need to be. There is no right or wrong, or predestined place or state you are trying to achieve. There is only the journey of becoming bigger in heart and spirit, and ever more beautifully your Self. And there is only the task and sacred responsibility of making the most stunning art you can with your one, wondrous life.

SPRING EQUINOX

Equal light and dark,
equal sorrow and joy.
From this Spring Equinox balance,
you step to the other side
of your story,
into the life and light
of new beginnings.

At the Spring Equinox, your journey of soul steps out of the darkness and into the light. On the Path of She, you descend into the sacred dark at the Fall Equinox, delving into its mysterious depths and engaging its trials and lessons in the months that follow. When the Spring Equinox arrives, it is time to leave behind your soul work in the belly of the dark, move past your old stories, and step into life-affirming new beginnings and personal growth.

In Nature, a new cycle of rebirth and growth begins as the Mother Earth draws life-inducing sunshine into the core of Her green bosom. Warming temperatures and increased rainfall rouse the dormant landscape. Seeds that have been gestating in the still, cold darkness send out green tendrils that break through the softening soil. Birds are returning from their migration, animals shed their winter coats and patterns, and fresh winds carry the evocative scents of new buds and green-growing things.

Easter coincides with the Spring Equinox. Both its religious roots as a celebration of the death and resurrection of Christ, and the secular traditions of the Easter bunny and eggs speak of springtime themes of rebirth and new beginnings. Spring fever is spreading, firing us up to clean our home, dig up and plant our garden, and embark on new projects and adventures.

We reconnect with Persephone's story at the Spring Equinox. She began Her journey in the Underworld at the Fall Equinox, and now She rejoins Her Mother Demeter in the sunlit realm of Spring. We know Demeter through Greek mythology, with Her gifts of agriculture and grain. But Her deepest gift is the promise of renewal and rebirth.

For millennia, Demeter and Persephone have carved the

path of our human spiritual evolution through their tale of descent into darkness and death, and return to light and life. Persephone, through Her travels and trials, cultivates a far-reaching maturity that can bridge and contain the opposing energies of the death-centered Underworld and the life-centered realm of Demeter. She returns to Her Mother as a feminine power in Her own right, Queen of the Underworld and Goddess of spring growth.

In this ancient tale and the natural world, the Spring Equinox brings together a powerful convergence of dark, light, death, life, old patterns and new possibilities that are held in balance before the scales tip in favor of light and life. New growth is not separate from the darkness, death, trials and sorrows from which it emerges. Green-growing things root themselves in the composting soil, made richer from death and decay, as they reach upward to the sun-bright sky; all these things nourish the new-budding life. So too Persephone comes into Her full power and maturity by balancing and containing the energies of the Underworld and the sunlit realm, and in doing so She returns springtime to the land above.

You are not separate from these primal mysteries and immense forces. The Spring Equinox offers a moment to reflect upon and embrace the opposing energies that infuse and inform your journey of soul: inner and outer, darkness and light, life and death, beauty and wounding, and joy and sorrow. It asks you to cultivate a state of balance and equanimity that roots your new, life-affirming growth in the trials and lessons of your old stories. In these ways, you follow in Persephone's footsteps, a presence and power in your own right as you step from the darkness into the light, and into the welcoming, waiting arms of the Great Mother and your sacred feminine heritage.

A Sabbat Mystery
Demeter and Our Spiritual Evolution

At the portal where the Underworld opens to the sunlit realm, the Goddess Demeter waits for you, just as She has waited for Persephone from time immemorial. She is queenly in bearing and stature, clothed in a flowing gown of warm browns and soft greens, the colors of the good green Earth. Her raven-hued tresses, faintly streaked with silver gray, smell fresh and fragrant, like rain-washed wildflowers. Though She smiles warmly in welcome, Her eyes, the blue-black of a stormy sea, hold a great sorrow in their depths, and a great love.

One of your feet is still upon the cold, stone stairway that descends into the dark below, and the other touches the downy, green surface of Spring's first grass. Both places lay claim to you: the Underworld with its mysteries and trials of darkness, sorrow and death, and the sunlit realm with its life-giving energies of light, joy and new growth.

Demeter reaches out a hand and pulls you upward into a mother's embrace, tight and loving, with no separation between your two beating hearts. Then She takes your face between Her warm palms, gazing deep into your eyes and unearthing what you are made of and how you have changed since the last time She beheld your soul.

"Here, in the sweet-scented land of Spring," Demeter says, "I have celebrated my daughter Persephone's return from the depths of the Underworld. And here, I have long waited for this moment when you and your human kin would find your way back to my side and the ways of the Greater Mother.

"Come, there are mysteries I would share with you so you will know the import of this turning point on your journey of soul, and in this Great

Turning in the spiritual unfolding of humankind."

Demeter leads you away from the biting drafts that reach upward from the belly of the Underworld, and draws you deeper into the sunlit meadow, enlivened with bright clusters of spring flowers and the sounds of insects, birds and other wild things. You sit beside each other, with the green earth beneath you, the blue sky above, and the winds blowing fresh and balmy.

"When the world was young, there was no separation between humanity and the Great Mother," Demeter begins, "Your primal ancestors lived in harmony with Her life-centered ways, just as Persephone stayed close by my side, and I protected and cared for Her, keeping Her out of harm's way.

"Yet there comes a time when children must leave the circle of their mother's love and find their way in the world on their own terms. Persephone left me to descend into the Underworld realm of darkness and death, and your ancestors turned away from the Great Mother and descended into a grievous period of your history. And so a long, cold Winter came to the Earth, where dominion and death overruled the creation and nurturance of life as the bedrock of your human society, and I mourned the loss of my daughter and the immense suffering of the Great Mother's children."

As Demeter speaks, you walk beside Her in Her remembrances, witnessing this long winter through Her tear-filled eyes and sorrowful heart. Long She wandered the world searching for Her daughter, and long She beheld the atrocities committed by humankind against each other and the living Earth. And as you walk with Demeter, the restless ancestors gather round you, victim and perpetrator alike, caught in the web of destruction and despair of this old tale, woven of our worst instincts of fear, greed, hatred and will to power.

Without words, you understand that our modern reality is a continuation of our ancestors' lives, where our shadow overrides our light in a great imbalance between the worst and best of our human nature, and that the pain of your personal story has its roots in this much older tale.

"Yet as the seasons of the Earth turn, so do the seasons of humanity," Demeter continues, "Many powers are converging, within and without, to wake humanity from its long winter of soul. Spring is in the air; Persephone walks the land above; and here you are, by my side, reaching for the ways of the Great Mother once more."

"In this awakening and Great Turning, Persephone is your teacher. She sought out Her wholeness in the belly of the Underworld, willingly suffering its trials and lessons to test and come to know Herself in the fullness of Her being. By these travels, Her power and selfhood were honed, and She returned to me maiden no longer, but Goddess and Queen in Her own right.

"So too humankind has lived the full range of its nature, both the shadow and light, and horror and beauty. As you individually and collectively emerge from your travels in the Underworld of humanity's shadow-side, you can follow Persephone's example. You can become powerful and wise enough to embrace the breadth of your human nature, ancestral heritage and life experiences — the good with the bad, and the shadow with the light — and in doing so, you become a child no more, but a person honed and matured by your trials and lessons."

In the warm circle of Demeter's mother love and wise words, the cold grip of Her remembrances and the lingering despair of the ancestors begin to fade, calling you back to the springtime brilliance of the surrounding meadow. Whatever pain you feel or burden you carry from your personal and ancestral stories have brought you to this evolutionary cusp. You need not be trapped by a past that no longer serves you; instead you can use its trials and lessons to fuel your journey of soul, and help you step out of this old tale and your own old story, and into a fresh new beginning.

"It is time for we ancient ones to find our rest," Demeter says, "Humanity's long winter of soul is ending. The ancestors' stories are done. They have served their purpose of bringing you to this evolutionary, awakening moment of choosing the Great Mother's life-centered ethos once more, from a place of power and wisdom. We pass this blessed world on to you. What comes next will be of your choosing and making.

"Let your suffering be the compost that feeds your new growth, and let your joy draw your hungry limbs upward to embrace life. Trust yourself. Trust each other. Begin again."

Demeter smiles and runs a single finger along the contours of your face, as if to memorize its cherished details. Then She fades into the green meadow and clear, blue, cloudless sky. Bird song fills the air. The tips of nearby branches sport the brownish-green of new-formed buds. The air is still, warm and sweet.

Freshly emerged from the Underworld into the sunlit realm, you bridge the divide between what was and what can be. Fill yourself with Demeter's wise words and Persephone's powerful teachings; know that this is truly a turning moment in your spiritual evolution and that of our human species. Then give yourself over to the primal promptings of Spring. Turn your face back to the life-affirming ways of the Great Mother. Commit to cultivate the change that will help new growth emerge from the rich compost that is your life and ancestral heritage.

Don't disappoint Demeter. She has left this precious world

in your trembling hands.

A Sabbat Teaching
Equanimity in Motion

At the Spring Equinox, we honor this time of equal light and dark, and equal sorrow and joy.

Darkness, sorrow and death have their place in the natural cycle of things, as do light, joy and birth. The wild realm reflects this truth as it morphs its way through the shifting seasons. But we humans can dig in our heels, clinging to darkness and sorrow, grasping at light and joy, and tipping easily in one direction or the other.

Where is our equanimity, our balance? When is it time to turn our focus inward, to darkness, sorrow and death-like endings? When do we leave these things behind and truly bask in light, joy and the wonder of new beginnings? How do we learn to ride the seasons of our life as effortless and gorgeously as the green-growing world?

Outside my window, sunlight filters through evergreen branches, casting a luminescent-green hue over my woodland viewscape. The answers to these questions are there, in the forest realm and the ways of Nature.

All things are present always. In the rich humus of the forest floor, death and life co-mingle. Seed cones lie side by side with rotting trunks. Layers upon layers of decomposing organic matter feed tiny saplings and towering elder trees. Roots dig deep into the dark belly of the Earth, while branches reach high into the sunlit skies. Night and day both govern the daily patterns of forest life.

We are no different. Parents age and leave this world as

their children bear children. Sorrow and loss help us love deeper and choose wiser; like compost they can enrich and feed our life experiences. Light and dark, sleeping and waking, introspection and action, govern the patterns of our everyday. All things are present always.

The forest is equanimity in motion. It is an ever-shifting balance of darkness and death with light and life. With the change of season, one state naturally steps into the foreground as the other recedes, but neither ever totally replaces the other, and both are absolutely interdependent.

Our life is a shifting balance of personal seasons. There will be times when darkness, sorrow and death need to be in the foreground, but light, joy and life are present too, holding and softening our suffering. And other times, when the sun is shining bright and life is good and delicious, and we need to give ourselves over to these wonders, knowing that our sorrows and challenges make the high points all the more poignant and precious.

Nothing we are going through will last forever, nor will it be forgotten. Our life is woven of light and dark, and joy and sorrow; it is made up of death and birth moments. All these things are equally present, equally essential, though in different measures at different times. They make us strong, resilient, complex and wise. By accepting these truths and letting them guide us, we can find our balance; we can become equanimity in motion.

Guided Meditation
Power and Presence of Balance

On the day of the Spring Equinox, settle yourself in a private place in your home where you won't be disturbed. Open the window to let in the fresh spring air. Close your eyes and consciously use your breath to loosen and relax your body.

Shift your focus to different parts of your body and imagine your breath moving with your awareness, infusing your muscles and loosening your joints until they feel supple and open: start with your feet and legs; move up to the base of your spine, hip cradle and sex; then to your solar plexus and belly region; next focus on your heart, chest cavity and mid-back; then your shoulders and down through your arms and hands; back up to your throat, jaw and face; and lastly around the back and top of your head. When you are done, return your focus and breath to the center of your body, anchoring in your core and emptying your mind of any remaining thoughts or stress.

From this anchored, supple place, imagine yourself at the portal where the Underworld opens into the landscape above. Spring has come and it is time to return to the sunlit world; you stand poised with one foot in the realm of darkness and death, and the other in the land of light and life. Sense the push and pull of these primal, opposing energies on your psyche, and any discomfort or excitement this elicits in you. Then take your next step and fully emerge from the Underworld into the life-giving powers of bright sunshine and warmth.

Take in the immense symbolism and import of this moment. You are stepping out of your Underworld trials and sorrows, past the burdens and constraints of your old story, ancestral heritage and our human shadow-side, and stepping into the life-affirming energies of the Great Mother and sacred feminine. And in making this shift, you are part of a greater transformation that extends to all of humanity and our Earth home.

In whatever way this resonates with you, and where you are

on your journey of soul, feel the power of this moment, inside of you, outside of you, and in the listening, waiting Cosmos.

Now imagine Demeter waiting for you, just as She has waited for Her daughter Persephone. See Her as Goddess and Earth Mother, in Her immense power, strength and queenly beauty. Let Her enfold you in a motherly embrace, knowing that you are Her beloved child, returned to Her side after your long journey of trials and sorrows. Draw in Her living-earth scents, life-affirming energies and Her infinite love. Share whatever words of connection and reunion arise between you.

Demeter has come to guide your transition to the other side of your story. Like Persephone, you need to become powerful and wise enough to bridge and balance the complexities and polarities of your nature and life story. You can only learn this equanimity through experience. At the Spring Equinox, Mother Nature can be your greatest teacher as She balances the immense energies of darkness, death, light and life in service of renewal and rebirth.

Clasp Demeter's hand and join your consciousness with Hers as She takes you far, far upward — past the swaying treetops and the deep-blue sky — beyond the outer limits of our atmosphere — into the cosmic dance of Earth, moon and sun. Witness this wondrous dance, with its perfect balance of night and day, and dark and light, taking just a tiny drop of its vastness inside of you.

Ride these mighty influences back down to the Earth's surface, where the kiss of sunlight coaxes seedlings to cast off their winter rest and send out their tender shoots of new growth. Dive into the dark underside of the soil, where beetles, worms and microbes mix the compost of decomposing matter that nourishes the living land. Sense the lingering clutch of Winter in the deep digging roots of the trees. Again, take a tiny drop of this vast complexity inside of you.

Then follow Demeter's awareness as it enters your inner landscape, revealing these same mysteries and complexities within you.

Sense the energetic tug of Earth, moon and sun on your flesh. Feel the equal presence of day and night, and light and dark on your psyche and core body patterns. Take in the quickening pulse of Spring coursing through your veins, enticing you with the thrill of new possibilities. Open to your own dark underside that holds your losses and suffering, and imagine it as rich compost that nourishes and guides the new growth emerging from within you. Feel the cold, wounded places inside of you that don't want to let go and seek to cleave you to their long winter of soul.

Meld with Demeter's bigness of being that can contain and balance all of these energies and impulses, and open to this same bigness within you. Like Demeter, like Persephone, like Nature, you are equally woven of darkness, death, light and life, and also your human experiences of stagnation, growth, beauty, wounding, sorrow and joy.

This bigness of being is equanimity in motion. And it is this state that can take you to the other side of your story and the spiritual evolution that awaits you there.

Breathe this experience of equanimity and balance into the core of your being. Let it shift and rearrange your current state of mind to help you feel more self-acceptance and peace with the complexities and polarities of your own life story and pathwork at this moment on your journey of soul. Take your time, and lots of deep breaths, until you find your inner state of equanimity and balance.

Then gently separate your consciousness from Demeter's.

Use your breath to sink back into your personal center and field of awareness.

Demeter turns to face you. Gaze into each other's eyes. See yourself through Her loving heart and presence. Know that She bears witness to your struggles, your strength and the hard work you have faced to come to this transformative moment. Drink in Her trust and belief in you. Take all of this mother love inside of you, and trust and believe in yourself. Express your deep gratitude for Her guidance and say goodbye. And then, in a heartbeat, She is gone.

Though you stand alone at this portal, with the spring landscape before you and the Underworld at your back, you are also not alone. Demeter's wisdom, love and belief in you, Her beloved child and a child of the Great Mother, shine bright in your living body.

It is time to return to the waking world, bringing this vast experience of equanimity and balance with you. Use your breath to anchor your awareness in your physical body. When you feel yourself fully returned to the sunlit reality of your everyday life, settle inside yourself and notice that something has changed. You are on the other side of your own story, with the powers of life compelling you forward into the spring of a wondrous new beginning.

Inner Pathwork
The Middle Path of Equanimity

Equanimity is closely allied with the concept of the middle path that Hecate spoke of in the Samhain Sabbat Mystery. The middle path asks you to consciously engage the full breadth of your life story and pathwork: the light, shadow, beauty, wounding, joy and sorrow. Equanimity helps you to cultivate the balance and neutrality needed to embrace and integrate these complex, divergent aspects of your personal makeup and life experiences.

The middle path and equanimity are both essential to your journey of soul. When you find yourself on the other side of your old story, this doesn't mean that the difficult and wounded parts of your life go away, or that you are done with pain, sorrow and healing work.

What it does mean is that you have become a different person, and that you engage the full expanse of your pathwork from a place of self-awareness, power, wisdom, balance and neutrality — the markers of equanimity and the middle path.

Neither the middle path nor equanimity comes easy. Most people are more comfortable with either-or, good-bad dualistic ways of thinking, and it can feel very disconcerting to hold opposing, sometimes paradoxical ideas and energies at the same time. Yet, with practice, you can train yourself to think and process in these powerful ways.

Your guided meditation gave you a taste of the equanimity of Nature and its mirror reflection within you. This inner pathwork exercise can help you build on your mediation experience through further exploration and practice.

Start by imagining your journey of soul through the lens of Persephone's return from the Underworld to the sunlit realm. You too have been traveling the Underworld, struggling with your pain and suffering, stirring up your hidden desires, discovering the seeds of your beauty and wounding, and dancing with the mysteries that underlie everyday reality. However you have experienced these things through your previous Sabbat pathwork and on your journey of soul, call these energies and remembrances to you, with the intention of doing this work in alignment with your highest good at this time.

Now imagine yourself poised to return to the sunlit realm, bringing your Underworld experiences with you. Use your breath to enter even deeper inside this imagining. Open yourself to the polar energies that are present for you in this moment. Feel the push and pull of death and life, shadow and light, and wounding and beauty as you have experienced them through your pathwork. Sense the winter-like grip of your fear and resistance, and your desire and exhilaration in the face of the alluring possibilities of new growth and positive change.

Don't try to block or tame your discomfort or your excitement. Just be present and bear witness to your current state of mind and your ability to navigate these big, messy forces as you fully emerge from the Underworld. This neutral, open place is equanimity.

Now make this experience more concrete. Choose one simple, specific, positive thing that you would like to nurture and grow in your life right now. On a piece of paper, draw a chart with two columns. In one column, write down the key reasons why you want to change in this way and its positive impacts on your life. In the other column, record the key reasons you want things to stay as they are and the negative effects of making this change.

Don't get caught up in your emotional reactions, and don't analyze or judge what is showing up on your list. Stay neutral and be completely honest with yourself. When you are done, read the list over and then look deep inside yourself to see if there is anything essential you have missed or something that you are resistant to name and include. Write these things down as well.

Then put the list to one side, but carry the energy of the two columns inside of you for the next several days. Again, resist judging, analyzing or making comparisons with the data you've recorded. The intent of this exercise is for you to experience stretching your psyche to hold two conflicting positions at the same time. Allow yourself to feel the discomfort and tension of this polarity, without pushing anything away, problem solving or looking for resolution. This is the middle path. Your ability to remain balanced and open in the face of these conflicting positions is your equanimity.

Let right action come to you of its own accord, with minimal mental effort on your part. If this doesn't happen within the time you've allotted for this exercise, let the whole thing go and wait for it to resolve itself. There is tremendous power in the meeting and mixing of opposite energies that allows something new and unexpected to organically emerge, and tremendous personal development in being able to stay in a place of equanimity without the need to push for answers and solutions.

Keep practicing these skills with simple situations that you can easily wrap your mind around, not just in your spiritual pathwork but also in your everyday life. Then work your way up to more complex and emotionally demanding issues. In these ways, you can continue to cultivate your equanimity, develop your capacity to walk the middle path, and integrate these potent skills into your life on the other side of your story.

Outer Pathwork
The Garden of Your Life

Our Deep Self responds to the primal promptings of Spring. We sense an inner quickening in the presence of chartreuse buds, warm, freshening breezes, and the amorous, vocal courting of birds. Things deep within us start to reach outward, seeking their place in the sunlit realm of our everyday life.

In your inner pathwork exercise, you have started to explore your impetus for new growth by considering a simple, positive change you would like to nurture and grow in your life. Now expand this exploration by listening closely to the quiet, timid whispers inside of you that spur you to take your life in a new direction or pursue a latent talent or passion — the secret desires you push down as impractical or terrifying. Gather them close as the precious messengers of soul that they are. Sense which one of these soul-sourced desires wants to bubble up to the surface, and makes your heart beat faster. Imagine this desire as a tendril of new growth that can take you closer to the life you are longing for.

Name this tender new shoot and the specific changes it suggests. Explore its connections to the seeds of your beauty and wounding that you've encountered in your previous Sabbat pathwork. How is it linked to your beauty and best qualities? How can it heal and transform your old stories and wounded places? How would your life be different, better, if this new growth takes root and flourishes in your outer existence? How can these changes help take you to the other side of your old story and patterns, and move you forward into a positive new beginning?

It's not enough to just know what you want to change, you also have to take concrete steps to manifest new possibilities. Think of your outer life as a garden that has lain fallow during the winter months. If you want something new to grow, you need to prepare your garden space.

Develop a plan for preparing the garden of your life for this soul-sourced tendril of new growth. What must be cleared away to make room for this new growth? What basic life changes are needed to facilitate its rooting and flourishing? Are there parts of your life that already support these changes, or that will dampen and resist them? How can your old story and sorrows inform and nourish your new choices and actions? What practical considerations and challenges do you need to address with your plan? What resources, inner and outer, need to be in place to help you tend and enliven this new growth?

Translate your answers to these questions into a plan with steps and timeframes for preparing your outer life to facilitate and nurture this new growth. With your plan, remember that you can take things one step at a time, learning and adjusting the next steps as you go. But taking that first step is essential, and you must do so with the full knowledge that change is never easy, and never comes without firm resolve, toil and sweat. In the spirit and energy of the Spring Equinox, it's time to get the garden of your life ready for the good things to come.

Walk the Path
Pebbles and Avalanches

Demeter's message is clear: great change is afoot; humanity has reached a crucial turning point and we must step past our old stories, heal our lives, transform our human ways and begin anew. In the symbolism of the Spring Equinox, it is time to leave behind the long winter of our soul and return to the life-giving powers of the sunlit realm.

Your Spring Equinox meditation and pathwork asked you to step through to the other side of your story, cultivate equanimity and prepare your life for new growth. In plain language, you are being asked to profoundly transform your life in positive new directions.

But change is never easy, and sometimes any kind of external indication of internal change can feel daunting. You may want to keep your healing and personal growth private, or fear that it may threaten the outer elements of your life, such as your family, job and relationships.

The profound transformation being asked of you in the Spring Equinox Sabbat Mystery, Teaching and pathwork may seem overwhelming. How do you step to the other side of your old story and the shadow-side of our collective humanity? How do you become as powerful and present as Persephone in the face of all that life throws your way? How do you develop the sophisticated, demanding skills of equanimity and walking the middle path? How do you prepare and change your life to cultivate positive new growth? How do you play a constructive role in shifting our messy, destructive human society in a more life-affirming direction?

The answer to all these questions is simply that you start with wherever you are right now, in whatever way makes sense to you. Your life will reveal your current pathwork and way forward, small change by small change. A well-positioned pebble can start an avalanche. Transformative change is no different. Small changes, in the right direction, can get bigger things moving.

Our soul speaks in the language of symbols, and our body responds to physical, sensual objects. When you make a physical change in your life, even one that seems small, you are activating deeper forces held within your body and soul, and aligning them to a common purpose — a pebble of choice or action that can bring about an avalanche of transformative change.

The pathwork exercises purposely ask you to keep things simple and small. The inner pathwork exercise suggests focusing on a simple, specific change when practicing the demanding skills of equanimity and walking the middle path. The outer pathwork exercise recommends that you take one step at a time when preparing your outer life for change and new growth.

In the weeks that follow, as you continue to practice these new skills and make positive, soul-sourced changes in your life, keep the principle of pebbles and avalanches in mind. You don't need to make a public declaration or dramatic alterations in your life. Your choices and actions can be small ones — pebbles of change that have potent meaning for you but aren't necessarily highly visible to others or radical shifts in your life. Perhaps it is a piece of jewelry, a new color added to your wardrobe, a journal book, a beautiful object or work of art, or a change in diet or habit. It doesn't matter what it is, as long as it is symbolic of your new life direction, and feels positive and empowering to you.

Let each small, symbolic change naturally unfold into other changes, all held within the greater intention of cultivating the life you most deeply desire and of growing in positive, life-affirming directions. Trust yourself, stay true to this intention, work hard, become ever more strong, resilient and wise, and Spring Equinox's promise of rebirth and new beginnings will come, not just in your personal life, but in your circles of family and community, and out into the greater world of our shared humanity.

BELTANE

In the heated passion that is Beltane,
offer up your essence
and beauty
to the wild, fertile juices
of Creation.
Be a lover of life,
within and without.

At Beltane, your journey of soul is all about embracing the delicious, transformative energies of the wild world. Now is the time to surrender to your innate, powerful desire to make love and make life, and to bud and flourish in the sunlit realm from the essence and beauty of your Deep Self.

You need only look to Nature to awaken and fuel this sacred longing inside of you. The cold, death state of Winter has been long forgotten and the powers of life and light are turned on high.

The green world is in the midst of a love-fest, displaying its erotic, fertile impulses with brazen exuberance: the brilliant green of new foliage, the mating rituals of birds and beasts, and the profusion of airborne pollen.

May Day is the secular celebration of Beltane, with its traditional maypole dance. A tall pole is planted in the earth and decorated with flowers and long ribbons. Dancers, each holding a ribbon, circle the pole in opposite directions while interweaving their ribbons. This lovely and seemingly innocent custom has its roots in Beltane's sexual, fecund energies. The maypole is a giant phallic symbol arising from the fertile earth, and the two weaving ribbons represent sexual union and the creation of new life.

The Green Man is the God that beckons us at Beltane. He is the guardian of the wild world, and the master of the mysteries of life and creation. With the veil between the worlds thin, the Green Man walks the land, leaving a trail of burgeoning life in His wake. His touch is a quickening magic that spreads like wildfire, igniting the hungry impulse of life to create new life. All living things, including humankind, are beholden to the Green Man's powers.

When you step into the Green Man's magic, you enter His dream of light, love and life-making. He embraces you as lover in the gorgeous, ever-unfolding dance of co-creation, with your outer existence arising from the wellspring of your unique essence. The Green Man's dream runs counter to the repressive, life-fearing ethos of our modern society that strives to domesticate your wild instincts and entrap you in a limited, self-negating worldview.

Beltane, like Samhain, is an edgy Sabbat, stirring up primal forces that have long been denied and suppressed in our human psyche. As Samhain calls us to be wide open and raw in the face of death and endings, Beltane calls us to be naked and uninhibited in our lover's embrace of life. Of the two Sabbats, Beltane can be the most challenging because it takes us up against our personal wounding and societal prohibitions that negate and distort our desires, sensuality and sexuality.

Though honoring and healing your wounding are essential to your Path of She pathwork, for everything there is a season. At Beltane, you step away from your wounding, embrace your soul's desire for beauty and new growth, and give yourself over to the life-creating-life drives that permeate this Sabbat. Let the Green Man and wild realm teach you about transformative change, where immense beauty and new growth naturally emerge from the old and stagnant to heal and renew your life and our world.

A Sabbat Mystery
The Green Man and the Dance of Life-Making

At the edge of the forest, haloed in the chartreuse brilliance of backlit foliage, the Green Man awaits you. He is a lean, powerfully built man, dressed in Lincoln green, with penetrating chestnut-brown eyes and a captivating smile. With a crook of

His finger, He beckons you to join Him.

Without a word, the Green Man leads you deeper into the forest. As He walks, an aura of light and heat radiates outward from His body, firing up everything within His circle of magnetism. Unseen creatures scent the air with the feral musk of mating, trees release yellow dustings of pollen, wildflowers burst into bloom, and baby chicks break through their eggshells.

Something delicious stirs within you, a mirror heat that fires up your core and loosens the fibers of your being. Your inhibitions melt away, overrun by a primal desire to take the untamed, fertile life force of this mysterious Green Man inside of you.

This urge is not so much about sex, though it may feel similar in your body. It rises from the most sacred, secret places inside of you, reaching out to make love and make life from the very essence of your soul.

The Green Man turns to you, His face suffused with passion and love. He places His hand on your mid-body and an intense, thrumming current runs between you. Within your core, something pushes past the stagnant, blocked places inside of you as tendrils of new growth unfurl and reach hungrily toward the Green Man's magnetic touch.

"Your hunger and my hunger are one," He says, His voice rich and husky, "your deepest beauty longs for expression in the outer world, and the outer world longs for your deepest beauty. My quickening magic can ignite your sacred hunger and make fertile your flourishing in the sunlit realm. Is this what you desire?"

With your yes, the Green Man transforms into a being woven of shimmering luminescence. His living-light body pushes up against your outer form, insistent and irresistible, and you open yourself wide to His luscious, energetic embrace. Together you tumble deeper into His wild-world dream of rutting and nesting and the pushing forth of life. One heart, one breath, one ecstatic force unite you, the Green Man, the forest plants and creatures, and every living being of the Earth, in the irrepressible drive of life to create new life.

In this glorious embrace, all traces of the waking dream of the human world melt away: your suppressive, domesticated ways that block your primal, wild instincts; your self-judgments and limitations; the outer voices that tell you who you are and how to live your life; and the destructive, life-fearing ethos that plagues human society. They are but distant memories, constructed by a shadow dream that has no sway in this other, more compelling and nourishing, wild-world dream.

Here there is only light, love and the Green Man's passionate imperative for every plant and creature to offer up the unique seeds of its essence and beauty to the magnificent, ever-changing melange of creation. With the Green Man's kiss, you give yourself over to your wild desire to live and flourish from your deepest essence and beauty, alongside the natural wonders of the Green Man's realm.

For what could be just one shining moment or a season of bliss, you revel in your life-making dance with the Green Man and the forest. Then your energies separate; He stands before you, returned to His physical form, and you find yourself, once more, on the edge of the forest.

"This wild-world dream we have shared is real, as is your hunger for your deepest beauty to have form and expression in the outer world. The life you are longing for has taken root in your inner landscape. Even now, its tendrils, infused with my quickening powers, are reaching for their place in the sunlit realm.

"Be warned and be wise. As you step back into the everyday that is your life, this dream will fade and the human dream will impose its order upon you, an order that denies my wild ways and debases the primal, creation impulses that run hot in your human blood. Forces, within and without, will resist this tender new growth within you.

"My magic serves you even in the face of this resistance. Remember your wild encounter with me and my forest realm. Remember the irrepressible drive of life to create new life that infuses every living thing. Be courageous, step away from the old stories that wish to bind these powerful impulses within you. Give yourself over to the hard, dedicated, wondrous work of tending and nurturing the new and beautiful that is yours alone to gift to the outer world. As the new takes root and flourishes, so the old atrophies and dies away.

"What happens next will unfold by your choice and actions. To transform the old, you must birth the new and offer up its gifts to the greater world. Choose to do this work and you will change your life and this world for the better."

One last time He kisses you, a soft brush of lips on your brow, and leans close to whisper in your ear, "at the edge of the wild, between the dreaming and the waking, you will find me, always, waiting to love you ever deeper in this dance of life-making."

Then the Green Man smiles His radiant smile and steps back between the trees as the forest vision dims and disappears. Though He is gone, His igniting touch has done its work, leaving you forever changed. The new, beautiful life you hunger for is budding within you, and it is time to give yourself over to tending its continued growth in your everyday existence. What the Green Man has kissed awake can never go back to sleep. For you, and all your human kin, are beholden to His mysterious dance of light, life and creation.

A Sabbat Teaching
The Lover's Embrace of Life

Right now, in the heat of Beltane, the wild realm is expressing itself so loudly and so boldly that we just need to step out our door to receive its direct, powerful message: life is our ardent lover.

How can we doubt this in the light of life's wondrous love offerings: the hot kiss of sunshine on bare skin; dawn's glorious chorus of birdsong; a meadow blanket of wildflowers; the soft, sweet bite of a fresh-picked strawberry; the bubbling laughter of a toddling child; and the electric stroke of a lover's touch?

Our relationship with life is not monogamous; we share life's ardor with all growing things of this Earth. At Beltane, life comes courting, gathering every one of us into its lover's embrace. Sex and birth are everywhere — delicious, unstoppable, untameable — as plants, flowers, birds, bees and creatures, great and small, mingle, mate and burst forth new life in a stunning, overflowing brilliance.

These wild impulses run hot in our blood, no matter our attempts to block or deny them. We soften and open with the sensual tease of the strengthening sun. We delight in the enticing scents of unfurling buds of plant and flower. The primal juice of the creature realm sings to our creature flesh, awakening our feral instincts to make love and make life. And deeper still, life's lover powers stir the mysteries in the core of our being, igniting our hunger to birth and nurture our soul's latent desires.

Yet so much toxic debris blocks our lover's dance with

life. The shadow-side of our humanity represses, denies and distorts these powerful energies. Nowhere is our humanity more profoundly wounded than in our sensual, sexual, soulful life-creating-life drives.

Nature guides us always, even in the face of this terrible, damaging aspect of our personal stories and collective humanity. For everything there is a season: a time to seek our truth and healing in the winter-like grasp of our sorrow and pain, and a time to cast off the cold, deadening grip of our shadow-side and bask in the light and beauty of new growth and possibilities.

Of all of life's magnificent love offerings, the most miraculous is the gift of our Self. Every breath is a gift, as are the wonders of our spirit, mind and body. And with these precious gifts, we get to choose what we make with what we've been given.

Life is not a doting, benevolent lover. Everything in the wild realm has its seasons through death and darkness, life and light. We are no different.

New life emerges from stagnation and death. What is deep and beautiful in us arises out of our wounding and loss. Sometimes we have to hold on to these truths in the thick of our pain and sorrow. Sometimes we have to trust that the new that we long for is the true and best balm to what ails us. Sometimes, if only for a sun-bright season, we have to leave our hurt behind and give all we've got to tend and grow into the life we most dearly want to live. We can choose to dig deep, shine bright and make the most with what we've been given.

In these ways, we become the lover that returns life's embrace.

Guided Meditation

Lover of Your Life

On Beltane, in the heat of daylight hours, seek out a patch of the wild world where you can privately commune with Nature, preferably with soil at your feet and the sky overhead. Make sure this is a space where you feel safe and comfortable to go deep. If you can't be outdoors, settle yourself in front of an open window that lets in ample natural light and fresh air.

Close your eyes and use your breath to ground yourself. Track the soft, sensual rhythms of your breath, slow, slow in, slow, slow out. Savor the tingling passage of air through your nostrils, filling your lungs and stretching your muscles and ribs outward, and the long, gentle release of breath, flattening your belly inward toward your spine. Follow this pattern over and over, emptying yourself of thoughts and concerns, until your body feels supple, enervated and relaxed.

Focus your consciousness in your solar plexus and then reach your awareness and senses outward toward the exuberant ways in which Nature is bursting forth new life in your part of the world. With your eyes still closed, immerse yourself in the smells and sounds of the burgeoning life around you, and the wild-world energies of sex and birth; draw these energies into your body and let them connect you to the erotic, sensual currents that infuse the Green Man's Beltane magic.

Take a few minutes to check in with yourself in this exchange. Beltane energy is edgy and intense, and can sweep you off your center or dredge up any shame or wounding you may have around your body, sensuality and sexuality. Be very, very gentle and compassionate with yourself, and only take this work as deep as is good for you at this moment.

Yet do not retreat back into the shadowy places

in your psyche. For everything there is a season, and now is the time for you to embrace your life-making instincts for the new and beautiful to take root and flourish in your inner and outer landscapes. No matter your personal doubts, resistance and judgments, or those of others, know that life loves you as you are and longs for you to embrace and live from your deepest beauty.

Feel this powerful love and longing reaching for you, and sense your own hungry longing in response. Open to your primal desire to be part of this life-creating-life dance, and for your deepest essence and beauty to find form and expression in your outer existence. Let your wild instincts take over, surrender to this soul-based desire, and the Green Man will come to you.

Know that it makes no difference whether you are straight or gay, man, woman or transgendered, a blade of grass, a frog in heat or a nesting eagle — the Green Man is beloved and lover to us all.

In your inner landscape, let your wild instincts paint for you a forest wilderness decked out in its glorious, Beltane display of new growth: the bright, leaf-green canopy of trees, the musky scents of mating animals, and the melodic communion of nesting birds. Feel the heat rising from the soil, from the branches and foliage, and from the creatures of this place.

Feel a mirror heat emanating from your soul's desire. Surrender. Become the lover that says yes to life's embrace.

Imagine the Green Man emerging from between the trees. Take in His physical appearance, His scent and the way He moves His body. Feel how your body and heart respond to Him. Sense the energy field between you, and His magnetic pull on your body and soul. Share whatever words of welcome and communion come to you.

The Green Man is your lover. Open yourself wide — body, heart and soul — to His shining presence and power. Let Him in, let Him in, let Him in. Deeper, and deeper still, into the inner lattice of your cells where your life-light shines brightest.

Abandon yourself to the love- and life-making dance that arises between you. Whatever you need, in whatever form, the Green Man will give to you, for He is the lover-God whose ardor can spark new life and possibilities within you, rooted in your deepest essence and beauty.

Do not rush this embrace. Leave behind all traces of your old stories and hurts, and anything that stops you from being fully, wondrously present and sensually engaged. Luxuriate in His delicious companionship. Savor His taste of the wilderness and the delicious joining of your outer forms and inner energies. Let Him fill you, fill you, fill you, and receive His igniting, transforming magic with your whole being, making fertile your soul's desire to live and flourish from your Deep Self.

When this magical union feels complete, seal it with a sweet, gentle kiss. Then say goodbye to the Green Man with words of love and gratitude. Let the forest landscape fade away. Use your breath to bring you back into your physical body and waking reality. Slowly open your eyes to the bright light around you.

Do not doubt that you have been changed by this sacred union with the Green Man. But your work has just begun. Be warned and be wise; to change in soul-sourced ways takes courage and hard work. The shadow-side of humanity runs counter to the Green Man's magic, and you may come up against tender, wounded places inside yourself. These things may resist and block your impetus for new growth. So be gentle, take care of yourself, but do not let the old, stuck places hold sway on your journey of soul.

You must become the lover of your own life, tending your new growth, cultivating your deepest beauty, and making the most with what you have been given. It is time to dig deep, shine bright and embrace the magnificent gift that is your Self.

Inner Pathwork
The Two Faces of Desire

Desire plays a central role in our Beltane pathwork. To be clear, in the context of our journey of soul, this discussion of desire is not about our sexual urges or impulse to procreate. We are talking instead about our soul's desire to live from our Deep Self outward, with no separation between our true essence and beauty, and our everyday existence.

When allowed its natural, unencumbered flow, this soul-based desire cultivates the nourishing, powerful and joyful ways we engage ourselves and the outer world. Where we are blocked and cut off from our soul desire, its tremendous power becomes pooled, tangled and distorted. The natural becomes unnatural and toxic, manifesting in the malaise and dysfunction of our shadow desires: hungers, wants and impulses that neither feed our soul nor happiness, and bring discontent, negativity and imbalance to our life.

In your Green Man meditation, you embraced your desire to live and flourish from your deepest essence and beauty. To continue this transformative pathwork requires a clear understanding and conscious engagement of the two faces of desire: soul-based and shadow.

The intention of this exercise is to further explore the soul-based desire that fueled and inspired your Beltane meditation, including any shadow desires that may be triggered by this pathwork. As you do this introspection work, pay attention to anything that comes to you: words, emotions, images or sensations. But do not attach to or put meaning on the information you receive. Remain in an open state of curiosity and discovery.

This exercise can touch on painful, sensitive places within you, so only delve as deep as is good for you at this moment. And remember to practice self-care, ensuring you have the resources you need, inner and outer, to support your pathwork.

Use your breath to ground yourself in your body, and to still and quiet your mind. Settle into your inner landscape and open yourself to the desire that arose in your Beltane meditation. Start by asking yourself probing questions about the soul-based face of this desire. What are you longing to cultivate in your life? What inner beauty, personal gifts and qualities are linked to this desire? What new growth and personal change are being asked of you? What parts of your life would be affected by these changes?

As this information comes to you, let it paint a picture of what your life would look like if you embraced this desire. Make this picture as vivid as possible, sourcing from your inner knowing. Then step into this picture as if it is real. What emotions arise in you? What deep longings are being nourished? What positive impact would come from these changes, both for yourself and for others? Connect with the part of you that is a lover of life and give yourself over to this positive vision of your new life.

Continue this introspection exercise, but now focus on your shadow desires. Stay immersed in your vision of this new, positive life, and this time let your shadow-side speak. What are your gut-level, negative emotions and responses? What parts of this vision trigger your resistance? Where are you unwilling to change? What are your doubts and fears? Who and what in your outer life are going to oppose and block you? Imagine them speaking their opposition out loud. How do you respond to their words? How do their words reflect your own opposition and fears?

Now let this information paint a picture of what your life looks like with no change, leaving this soul-based desire unmet. How do you actively block and repress the expression of this desire in your everyday life? What beliefs and behaviors are involved? What parts of your life are negatively affected? What emotions arise in you? What wounded parts of your life story are triggered? Try to understand the deeper malaise and dysfunction that underlie this no-change vision, and their related hungers, wants and impulses. These are your shadow desires.

Rather than judge or push your shadow desires away, make them respected partners in your conscious change process. Your shadow desires mark the hurt, stuck places inside of you that need care and healing as you move forward in your personal growth. Pay attention to the information and insights that your shadow desires can reveal to you, and build this into your pathwork process.

Continue to deepen your understanding of your soul-based and shadow desires that came to you in this exercise. Align yourself with Beltane's irrepressible drive to create new life and beauty. Nurture the positive vision that arises from your soul-based desire. Acknowledge and include your shadow desires in your change process, with self-acceptance and compassion, but do not let these old parts of your story negate and block your pathwork. With love, tenderness and wisdom, the new that transforms you becomes the balm that heals you.

Outer Pathwork
Wired for Life

In our pathwork, we can become fixated on the negative, believing that we have to heal our pain, wounding and shadow-side before we can change for the better. Nature offers a different vision of transformative change. The impulse for new growth is hardwired into all forms of life. Maybe we can forget this physical reality in the dead of Winter, but not in the unruly fecundity of Beltane, with the wild world bursting forth in all its creation finery.

Like wild things, the core of our being is wired for life. When we grow in positive, new directions, change will come, and this change will naturally inform and transform our pain, wounding and shadow-side. Not necessarily in a linear, causal fashion, but what is old and stuck in us cannot help but be affected by the juice and energy of creation. This is the most profound magic of all.

In the spirit of Beltane, spend the next week indulging your wild-world instincts for positive growth and creative change. Write on a piece of paper: "I am wired for life." Pin this paper beside your bathroom mirror so you can see it first thing in the morning and last thing before you go to bed. Let these words be your mantra, awakening your desire for positive change and offering you an alternative lens for viewing your challenges.

Spend some time hanging out in the Green Man's world by going for a walk in your favorite wild space. Shift your awareness from your head to your body knowing, using your senses to connect and commune with the plant and creature inhabitants of this place. Be as silent and unobtrusive as you can. What attracts your attention? What do you find beautiful and intriguing? What smells are carried on the warm wind? What sounds permeate the space? What plants and animals cross your path? Close your eyes and sense the tingling brush of wild energies on your exposed skin.

Sink below the surface of physical form into the creation impulses that are turned on high in this season. The wild world is at one with its life-making drives and the quickening powers of Green Man magic. In your core, these same drives and powers speak to your living flesh and shining soul. Let your sensual, embodied exchanges with the plants, creatures and energies in this wild space loosen your limbs and unblock the flow of these forces within you.

Bring some of this wired-for-life, wild-world juice back into your everyday life. Take your cue from Nature's uninhibited indulgence of its sensual, creative impulses. Get a bit wild, step outside of your own skin, and experiment with something new and positive that you'd like to bring into your life. It doesn't have to be anything huge and life-changing. But choose something that is concrete, sensual and delicious.

Every time you start to dwell on something negative, remember your wired-for-life mantra and look for the positives. Ask yourself: what else is true in this situation? Where are the opportunities for healing and growth? How can I engage this situation from a place of empowerment, creativity and love of life?

At the end of the week, take a long look at the sign beside your bathroom mirror and a long look into your own eyes. Breathe in your experiences and insights from this week's exercise and let yourself truly know that you are wired for life. Every time you get a bit wild, try on something new and reframe your challenges as opportunities for growth, you are making the Green Man's magic of transformative change your own.

Walk the Path
The Delicious Factor

One undeniable feature of Beltane energy is that it is delicious. Nature is in a state of luscious abandonment to its love- and life-making impulses. Sensuality, sexuality, creativity, beauty, pleasure, these are things our body understands and craves. When we become a lover of life, giving ourselves over to these innate, delicious impulses — not as a hedonistic indulgence or an urge to procreate, but in service of our soul's longing to live in communion with the deep beauty inside and all around us — we can transform our life.

Delicious describes those exquisite moments when we are totally present and sensually engaged in our connection with our outer environment. It is our body's yum response to the smell of lilacs, a bite of bread fresh from the oven, the strong press of fingers on a stiff muscle, and the heated glance of a lover just before our bodies touch. It is the sparkle of our spirit when we laugh until our belly aches, lose ourselves in our favorite creative activity, gaze up into the fathomless wonders of a starlit sky, and witness the proud accomplishments of a special child. In these moments, our inside is at one with our outside, and we know that life is good.

The power of delicious should not be underrated. Though this power is most noticeable at Beltane, life is constantly inviting you to a full-body, full-senses engagement of the world around you.

When you embrace the delicious factor in your life, you are also saying yes to your wired-for-life potency (as explored in the outer pathwork exercise) that loosens and unblocks your inner, stuck places, and activates your innate instincts for positive growth and creative change.

In your Beltane meditation and inner pathwork, you have begun the courageous, transformative work of activating and exploring your soul-based desire to live and flourish from your deepest essence and beauty. In the weeks that follow, continue the challenging, wondrous tasks of cultivating your beauty, tending your new growth and living from the inside-out of your Deep Self.

As you actively engage your soul-based desire, you will most likely trigger the shadow desires of your inner wounded places, and come up against our societal shadow-side that denies and distorts your sensual, soulful, life-creating-life instincts. These shadow elements are also part of your pathwork that need to be embraced with compassion, tenderness, wisdom and self-care. Yet it is imperative to not let your shadow-based pathwork block or negate your essential tasks of tending and nurturing the new and beautiful in your life.

Make it a part of your pathwork to consciously step beyond your old stories and patterns of wounding and the repressive, domesticating ways of our culture, and to step into your natural, delicious impulses for pleasure, sensuality, creativity and positive engagement of your outer environment. Get a bit wild, try on novel, life-affirming options, and look for the silver linings of personal healing and growth when life challenges you. Trust that when life feels good, life is good, and when life feels bad, you can source its goodness to guide and empower your journey of soul. The new that transforms you can also be the balm that heals you and our collective humanity.

SUMMER SOLSTICE

Shine bright
and give generously,
from the blossoming beauty
that is you.
Nourish the hungry soul of this world
with your Summer
Solstice brilliance.

At the Summer Solstice, your journey of soul invites you to blossom, shining outward the true essence and beauty of your Deep Self into the sunlit world of your everyday life. Emulate Nature in this summer season of generosity and abundance by cultivating your soul-sourced authenticity and sharing your best gifts and qualities with others.

The Solstice marks the first day of Summer and a peak in the powers of light before the scales tip once more toward the dark. Nature grants us a heady display of its fully unfurled beauty and overflowing munificence. From the mighty oak tree with its vast, green canopy to the fledgling robin casting itself from the nest, what is inside — the unique, luminescent spark of Creation within each living being — seeks its destined place in the sunlit world.

Midsummer festivities are part of our ancestral heritage and are still celebrated around the world. Bonfires are lit, honoring the brilliance and fertility of the summer sun. Merriment, music, dancing and feasting abound, reminding us to take pleasure in the good things in life while the days are long and hot, and the natural realm shares its plenitude.

The life-centered ways of the Goddess and the sacred feminine are revealed in this plenitude. The Mother Earth holds us in Her loving, generous embrace, showering us with beauty and nourishment for our hungry bellies and souls. The Goddess is everywhere and in everything, calling forth the innate instinct within each living thing to blossom into the full expression of its true essence and purpose, in accordance with its unique place in the great weaving of life.

The robin cannot help but embrace its powers of flight,

navigating the air space on its outstretched wings. The oak cannot help but spring forth from the acorn, sending its brown roots earthward and its green arms skyward. We cannot help but reach for our place in the greater world, drawing on the essence and gifts of our Deep Self. We may repress and truncate this primal soul imperative, yet our innate, unquenchable desire to flourish in our own unique way remains, ready to bloom outward, in all its brilliance, into a waiting world.

At the Summer Solstice, the Divine power that waits for you is your own Goddess Self who holds your remembrance of the ways and mysteries of the sacred feminine. She resides within the core of your being, connecting you with your inherent, indisputable beauty, worthiness and sacred purpose. She will show you the parts of your beauty and purpose that are ready to blossom, and will guide your journey of soul as you cultivate this blossoming in your everyday life.

In reuniting with your Goddess Self, you are realigning your inner and outer landscapes with the ethos of abundance that comes from the Mother Earth and permeates the natural realm. When you offer your very best to the communal table of humanity, in a spirit of grace, goodness and generosity, you make abundance a real, substantive part of your life, family, workplace and community, and encourage others to do the same. From these small and big changes, an ethos of abundance can take root and flourish in our human society where there is enough love and nourishment to feed, mend and transform our lives and world.

A Sabbat Mystery
The Goddess Within

On the edge of waking, with your consciousness still immersed in the liquid energies of dreaming, She waits for you. She is a shining being, woven more of light than flesh. She does not speak, but reaches out a hand to you. As your fingers touch, a sense of familiarity floods through you, along with an immense hunger to commune with this strange, exquisite being.

A sunny wild space opens before you, carpeted with lush, green grass and strewn with liberal splashes of brightly colored wildflowers. Nearby, a wooded area of towering deciduous trees offers a shady retreat under its leafy canopy. The place is alive with birdsong, chittering squirrels, buzzing insects and the rustling sounds of larger mammals. A gentle wind carries the earthy, green-world scents of a wildscape basking in the heat of the summer sun.

When your companion speaks, it's as if the sun shines inside your belly, filling you with its beneficent rays, "We are surrounded by the ways of the sacred feminine as they unfold in Nature. Every living thing on this Earth has a place and purpose in the great weaving of life and cannot help but blossom into its full presence and beauty. Look closely at the wildness around you and see that the plants and creatures naturally embody this truth, each a seamless, essential part of a living, breathing wholeness."

Your vision shifts with Her words and you can see into the energetic patterns that underlie the physical forms around you. When you look at the red-breasted bird perched on a branch overhead, you see also the soft-blue egg from which it hatched, the cellular matter that produced this egg and bird, and the unique, luminescent spark of Creation at its core that holds its robin nature. As the robin breaks into its sweet, clear song, you sense that it is doing exactly what it is meant to be doing at the prime of its life, blossoming into and expressing its robin essence and purpose to a listening and receiving world.

As you wander this flourishing landscape, your awareness

shifts to the other wild inhabitants. From the bees busy gathering nectar, to the grazing deer, to the swaying canopy of giant maple trees, you take in this same, seamless connection between inner essence and outer form. A sense of rightness settles in your bones, that this is the way life is meant to be, with a place and purpose for everything within a grander reality.

"In the human world, you have abandoned the ways of the sacred feminine and its natural life drives," She says, *"Most people don't live connected to their essence; they don't bloom into a beautiful, full expression of themselves and their sacred purpose in life. Much of the unhappiness and destructive impulses of your species find their source in this core wounding."*

Let yourself feel the cold, hard truth of Her words. Sense the masks your wear and roles you inhabit in your everyday existence that disconnect you from your soul-sourced authenticity and purpose. Open to the unmet needs and longings that arise from your inner core, and your mirror responses of distress and sorrow. This is one way of living. There is another, the way of the sacred feminine, and you are surrounded by it at this very moment.

In this dream place between the worlds, align your life with the ways of the living Earth in its full-blossoming powers. Choose to let the robin be your teacher in these things, doing exactly what it is meant to be doing, from the depths of its robin nature. Choose to bloom into the true essence and purpose of your Deep Self in whatever way is good for you at this time in your life.

The meadow scene transforms into a garden that is your

inner sanctum and holy of holies. Beside you, your shining companion solidifies into a person of flesh. When you look into Her radiant face, you see your own sparkling eyes and smiling lips reflected back at you, but with a deeper presence and power that you may not yet recognize in yourself. She is your inner Goddess Self who holds your sacred feminine powers and knowing.

"In the depths of your inner landscape, there is no separation between you and your true essence and purpose," She says, "You have never really lost me, nor your connection to the mysteries of the sacred feminine and the living Earth. These things have always been waiting for your remembrance and conscious engagement. And it is these things that call you to take your place in the sunlit realm, and to live from your very best gifts and qualities in your everyday life. This is the rightness of being that you seek, and the part you can play in building a better, more beautiful and joyful world. You need to simply show up as your true, beautiful Self."

She takes your face in Her hands and places Her warm lips against yours, granting you a sweet, awakening kiss that dispels the shadows and doubts that separate you from Her brilliant presence. Your cadence of heartbeat and breath synchronize, and your two forms merge into one. Her mysteries are your mysteries. Her power is your power. Her voice is your voice. Her shining is your shining. There is no separation and never was.

As you leave this dream and wake into your everyday life, you bring these magical workings with you. Your radiant Goddess Self now shines through your eyes. She is awake inside of you, anchoring you firmly in the ways of the sacred feminine, and guiding your journey of soul as you step into your destined place in the great weaving of life.

A Sabbat Teaching
A Vision of Abundance

Our human world is stuck in a mindset of fear and scarcity. There is not enough food, water, wealth, power, status, beauty or love to go around. An ethos of scarcity breeds a reality of scarcity, with a grab-what-you-can social order that has little regard for our impact on each other or our Earth home. From this miserly place, our scarcity ethos bears the fruits of poverty, social injustice, war, overconsumption, environmental destruction, and the countless greedy, fearful ways we wreak havoc on others and our world.

The natural realm offers a simple, glorious counter-ethos: abundance. The wondrous thing is that this abundance exists now; we are already living within its loving, generous embrace. At no time is this truth more evident than at the Summer Solstice when the Mother Earth lavishes us with goodness and beauty for our hungry bellies and souls.

Bees are busy making honey from the sweet nectar of flowers. Flowers are scenting the air with their stunning blooms. Fruits are dripping from the branches, ripening in the heat of the summer sun. Farm stalls are overloaded with fresh-picked produce. These things are the gifts of the Earth, given with an overflowing, life-centered munificence.

This is not to say that Mother Earth is always gracious and generous. The seasons cycle through scarcity, decay and death, just as our lives are sometimes stricken with loss, illness and death. Nature also delivers up devastation and destruction in the form of hurricanes, earthquakes, droughts, wildfires and other natural disasters. Though humanity has played a role in the severity and frequency of ecological calamities, these things have always been part of the natural order and balance of physical reality.

Yet Nature always returns to life and abundance. And this abundance is not a fantasy. It is real and solid, woven of the raw elements of sun, soil, rain and seed. It springs from an instinctive generosity, an ethos of only taking what is truly needed, and of giving more rather than less. A little seed blossoms into a whole plant, or a bush, or a tree that proffers a plethora of foodstuff and the seeds of future plants and harvests. The pit of a single plum grows into a tree that year after year offers up its fruits for our tables.

Imagine choosing this ethos of abundance as a guiding force in your life: making this abundance real and solid through the raw elements of your grace, goodness and generosity; living in harmony with Nature by taking only what you truly need, and giving more of yourself rather than less; and standing by this ethos, trusting in the greater truth of abundance and generosity, when faced with hardship, disaster and loss.

Imagine conceiving this same abundance in our human world, where power, worthiness, love, joy and other markers of personal satisfaction and social value are infinite and available for all, in accordance with our true, individual needs.

Imagine embracing the notion that we each have gifts to offer, from the bounty of our best qualities, and that we bring these gifts to the communal table of humanity in a spirit of generosity — giving more and only taking what we need in return.

Imagine that we work together to combine the raw elements of this amazing human potential to solve the problems we've created economically, socially and environmentally.

Within an ethos of abundance, we trust that anything is possible if we stay committed to a life-centered munificence that includes our human and non-human kin, and if we choose to live in harmony and balance within the greater weaving of life.

Know that an ethos of abundance breeds a reality of abundance. Though we cannot make these choices and changes for others, we can begin to live this vision of abundance with ourselves, and within our families and communities. Through offering up the fruits of our personal bounty in a spirit of kindness, generosity and abundance for all, change can spread outward, inspiring others to act in kind. And in this way, our individual choices and actions can create a vision of abundance that can heal and transform our world.

Guided Meditation
Thou Art Goddess

In the midday brilliance of the Summer Solstice, find a comfortable place in your home by an open window or a private space outside to do your meditation. Bring your attention to your center and imagine breathing in and out from your solar plexus. Feel your belly rise and fall with the movements of your breath. Slow your breathing down and track its reflexive, rhythmic cycle from fullness to emptiness, fullness to emptiness, over and over until your body is relaxed, your mind is empty, and your consciousness is deeply anchored in your inner core.

With a soft-focused gaze, open to the signs of Summer in your part of the world: the dry heat, the sun-bright, green edges of leaves, the fragrant smells of flowers and grass, and the infinite other ways Mother Earth is blossoming around you. See what plant, bird or other wild thing catches your attention, and notice its beauty and behaviors. Know that this plant or creature is doing exactly what it is meant to do, in accordance with the blossoming instincts of its unique essence and purpose.

Close your eyes and use your breath to shift your awareness down through your flesh and bones, and into the depths of your inner landscape. Draw the enervating powers of sunlight deep inside of you and feel it spark your blossoming instincts.

Imagine these instincts morphing into a pathway that can direct you to your inner sanctum where your Goddess Self — She who holds your knowing of the sacred feminine — awaits you. Seek Her out and She will show you the parts of your beauty and purpose that are ready to blossom at this time. Set the intention to do this pathwork in alignment with your highest good.

Sense the soles of your feet against the contours of the earth and let the powerful presence of your Goddess Self lead you forward. As you travel, take in the state of this path. Is it smooth and well-tended, in a state of neglect and disrepair, or somewhere in between? Is your way free and clear, or blocked by debris and brambles? Are you beleaguered by limiting thoughts, doubts and fears? Or are you in sync with the natural state of abundance and grace that underlies this path?

Take a deep, full breath and accept that, whatever its condition, this is your path and way forward to your beauty and blossoming.

Feel the rightness of your desire to reclaim your destined place in the greater weaving of Mother Earth. Open to your longing to be reunited with your feminine wisdom and instincts that connect you with the mysteries of beauty, blossoming and sacred purpose. Listen for the beckoning voice of your Goddess Self. Try to catch Her scent on the wind. Surrender to Her magnetic power and you will be drawn to Her side.

You will know when you have reached the threshold of your inner sanctum; something deep inside will tell you: yes, this is it, this is my most private, sacred space. Take a few minutes to center yourself and ensure you are completely present, for this is a powerful moment — a homecoming and reclaiming of your holy of holies.

Then step past the threshold, enter this sacred space and meet your Goddess Self. Your inner sanctum may be a garden, a wild space, a special place from your life, or a landscape out of a dream. Look around you; take in the colors, scents, sounds and details. Let yourself be completely at home.

Your Goddess Self may look like you, or have Her own unique appearance. Bask in Her beauty and bright smile, absorbing the details of Her physical form and the up-close sensations of Her energetic presence. Open to your own energetic and emotional responses to this reunion and home-coming.

Reach out to your Goddess Self, clasping Her hands in yours. Look deep and long into each other's eyes. Let the love and goodness that you are, and that infuses all things, flow between you. Settle into this rightness that is you — this worthiness that is you — this beauty that is you — this power, mystery and presence that are you.

Ask your Goddess Self to show you the parts of your beauty and sacred purpose that are ready to bloom in the sunlit realm of your everyday life, and the pathwork that will cultivate this blossoming.

Spend as long as you need with your Goddess Self to renew your bond and receive Her guidance, insights and loving support. Follow Her into the deepest roots of your beauty, gifts and best qualities. Delve into the true essence and purpose of your Deep Self. See what parts of your beauty and purpose are ripe for blossoming, and what your emerging pathwork may look like. Explore together your shadow-side, fears and doubts that are also part of your pathwork.

Expand your shared awareness beyond your personal pathwork and story to your broader environment, including your family, workplace and community. Open to your Goddess Self's connection to the natural abundance of the sacred feminine and Mother Earth. Let Her reveal the beneficial impact you can have on your outer environment through your beauty and gifts, and how you can bring more grace, goodness and generosity to your life and to others.

If you are ready, say yes to your blossoming and the pathwork that has been revealed to you. If you are not ready, share whatever changes and commitments are right for you at this moment on your journey of soul.

Your time with your Goddess Self, for now, is done. Embrace Her and feel the immense power and love that flow between you. She is a part of you, always present, always remembering your true beauty, innate worthiness, and sacred purpose and place in the great weaving of life. Express your gratitude for Her presence and guidance, and then bid Her farewell.

Retrace your passage along the pathway that led to your inner sanctum. With each step and breath feel yourself return to your physical body and everyday consciousness. Open your eyes and connect once more with the summer-bright world, basking in Nature's generous gifts of sunlight, fresh air and green-growing things.

Place your hands on your solar plexus and savor this moment. There is no separation between you and your feminine wisdom, and there never was. Like the plants and creatures of the natural realm, you too have a luminescent spark of Creation in your core that holds the unique essence and sacred purpose of your Deep Self. There is a place for you in the great weaving of life, just waiting for the shining outward of your deepest beauty and gifts. In this shining, and your spirit of grace, goodness and generosity, you are naturally a part of the munificence of the Mother Earth, and naturally help to create an ethos of abundance in our human society. The Goddess is everywhere and in everything. Thou art Goddess.

Inner Pathwork
The Beauty You Are

When you look in the mirror, what is the first thing that pops into your head. Do you see beauty or flaws? Do you, like me, compare your present self to the beauty you were in the past? And then realize that in ten years from now, you will look back on this moment and mourn that you missed the beauty you are now.

We are all perfectly, imperfect creatures with our own unique essence and beauty that arise from who we are, deep and true, from the inside out.

At this exact moment, and every moment of our life, we are infinitely beautiful and infinitely worthy, regardless of external or self-imposed measures of worthiness. The dung beetle doesn't stop to measure its beauty and value against a wild rose. It goes about the business of being a dung beetle, in alignment with its perfect, dung beetle purpose and place within the great order of life on this Earth.

In the energy and spirit of the Summer Solstice, anchor yourself in the beauty that you are in this now moment.

Start by connecting with your true face, rather than the face you present to the world. Make sure that you have undisturbed time for this exercise, and use a hand mirror or a mirror you can sit in front of comfortably.

Take a few deep breaths, with your awareness centered in your solar plexus; follow the slow in and out movements of your breath until your mind is still and empty. Then look at your face in the mirror as if you've never seen it before. Forget all the external masks and roles that you define yourself by. Pretend that you know nothing about yourself, and then become curious as to who you really, truly are.

This is not a cocktail-party encounter, but a soul-level communion. Ask your Deep Self to come forward and reveal your true essence and beauty through your eyes and the contours and expressions of your face. If any judgments or negative thoughts intrude, or you hear the voice or opinions of another person, let them go and open your heart wider. Your intention is to come to know and fall in love with the beauty of your Deep Self.

Enjoy this communion in whatever form it shows up: thoughts, insights, body sensations, images and emotions. Stay open and make a strong connection.

Then turn your gaze inward. Contemplate your beauty and sacred purpose, as revealed to you in your Summer Solstice meditation. What are your best qualities and gifts? How are you expressing and sharing them with others? Do you let them flow freely in your life or do you repress and hide them? What is blocking or holding you back? How can you step more fully into your blossoming? What would this look like? How would it change your life? How do you imagine this impacting others around you?

Consider these questions as an ongoing inquiry, rather than expecting answers to come immediately. For the next week, continue the mirror exercise every morning when you first wake up and every night before you go to bed. Do a few anchoring breaths and then look at yourself in the mirror. Look past the surface details, external measures of beauty and inner-critic voices. Dive into the depths of who you truly are, shining through your eyes, your skin and your presence. Thou art Goddess, with a unique, luminescent spark of Creation nestled in your core.

Your pathwork of blossoming begins here, in this simple practice of connecting with and affirming the innate worthiness and beauty of your Deep Self. Your value is not determined by externally imposed or internally ingested yardsticks. You don't have to do anything or be anything to be worthy.

It doesn't matter whether you are just starting on your spiritual journey or are well on your way, or whether you struggle with self-worth or have come to a place of true self-understanding and love. It is the rare individual who doesn't grapple with these issues. Wherever you are on your path at this very moment is beautiful and perfect because your pathwork, like your personal essence, is uniquely yours.

Your blossoming matters; your beauty and gifts can positively affect your life and the lives of those around you. With every healing step you take toward reclaiming your unique essence and sacred purpose, you become more deeply and profoundly yourself, and that authentic, soul-sourced presence radiates outward as you touch others in your immediate environment, and they, in turn, touch others. So step fully into your blossoming and give generously from those gifts and qualities that are yours alone to offer up to the communal table of our humanity.

Outer Pathwork
A Waking Dream of Abundance

A friend's husband was diagnosed with terminal cancer and given a short period of time to live. It was the height of Summer and the natural realm was in full bloom. My friend would go outside and the clear-blue sky would call to her. She'd know that this was what her husband needed, draw the exact blue of the sky into herself, and then gift it to him energetically when she returned home. This became her healing practice, drawing on Nature's abundance and beauty, and transferring these energies to her ailing beloved. Although I can't say her actions were the sole cause of his healing, her man went into remission and is still alive over twenty years later.

An intriguing story with a profound message that is especially poignant at the Summer Solstice: abundance is not a fantasy. We are surrounded by an overflowing, life-centered munificence — a waking dream of abundance where everything we need is being generously gifted to us, if we only have eyes to see and a heart to receive.

Our social mindset is disconnected from Nature's abundance, operating from an ethos of scarcity and fear. Yet we need only shift our perspective to access an alternative viewpoint where abundance is real and ever-present in the fruits and beauty of the land, and in the subtler energies and mysteries that underlie our everyday, waking reality.

In this outer pathwork exercise, you can experience this alternative viewpoint for yourself by trying out my friend's healing practice with Nature's abundance. Perhaps someone close to you is ill or suffering, or there is a social issue that calls to your soul. Or maybe there is a part of you that blocks your personal growth and blossoming. Pick one issue or person to focus on in this exercise.

A cautionary note before you start: in sharing the story of my friend's healing practice for her husband, I am not suggesting that we can cure anybody at will, nor that it is our place or responsibility to intervene in the pathwork and healing process of others. This is an exercise in service, not in power or ego, and it is not meant as a substitute for other healing interventions.

To be of service, you must have permission to offer healing to another. If you choose to do this exercise for someone other than yourself, speak to him/her first to gain permission. If for some reason it's not possible or practical to do this directly, you can have this exchange on a soul level. Use your breath to anchor in your Deep Self, open yourself to the other person's Deep Self, and then seek his/her consent.

Once you have decided on the focus of this exercise, and gained consent if needed, set your intention and send it outward into the world, like a prayer. In this intention, speak to your desire to simply be a bridge that transfers energy and beauty to another (or yourself), in alignment with his/her (your) highest good at this time.

Then, as you go about your regular, daily life, widen your awareness to receive the gifts of the natural realm: what energies, visions and teachings are here for you or for others? See what draws your attention. Take these gifts into yourself and direct them where they are needed.

There is a final piece to this story of my friend's healing practice for her husband: she asked me to look deep inside this situation and see if there was anything else she needed to understand. What came to me was that she was living in a state of grace in which she could be a conduit for the natural generosity and abundance of life itself. I told her that there was grace in living and grace in dying, and that she should not attach to outcome but stay with the quality of love, presence and awareness that this situation asked of her and her husband. Bring this same state of grace to your outer pathwork exercise. Be a clear, pristine conduit for Nature's healing gifts. Stay centered, strong within yourself, and humble. Let things pass through you (unless you are directing the healing at yourself), without any additional meaning or judgment. Don't get trapped in the ego game of over-inflating your self-image as healer. And don't take on the energies or problems of another.

Most important, don't get attached to outcomes. In any healing situation, there are great mysteries at play, and sometimes a person's journey may include loss, illness and even death. There is grace in living and grace in dying. You can offer love and the gift of healing energies, but you cannot choose for another, nor impose your ideas and expectations. Respect the other person's boundaries and choices, just as you would want others to respect yours.

After you have spent a week immersed in this healing exercise with Nature's abundance, look inside yourself to see how your experiences have changed you. How have you been touched by the grace and generosity of Nature? How has this shifted your understanding and engagement of the world around you? How can you continue to be a bridge and conduit for the great abundance of the natural realm in your life and the lives of others?

Imagine a world that lives in accordance with Nature's state of grace and generosity: where scarcity is met with abundance, horror with beauty, pain with joy, and suffering with compassion; and where there is enough happiness, love, respect, nourishment, beauty and power for everyone and everything. Then shift into that state of grace and generosity, stretch out your hands and send this waking dream of abundance outward, like a prayer, into the suffering hearts of our human world.

Walk the Path

Strut Your Deep Self

The Summer Solstice is not a time for modesty. The wild world is not shy about its beauty and gifts. Plants and creatures are engaged in a no-holds-barred life-fest of blossoming and flourishing, each according to its unique essence, place and purpose in this glorious weaving of Mother Earth. Be it a rose or a robin or a bee or an oak tree, each is doing exactly what it was created to do, in a stunning display of overflowing, abundant, vibrant life.

In the weeks to come, emulate the wild world and don't be shy about your beauty and gifts. In your Summer Solstice meditation and inner pathwork, you have been exploring your beauty, gifts and sacred purpose, and committing to your pathwork of blossoming.

Now is the time to shift from introspection into action, and to shine your deepest beauty and gifts into the sun-bright world. So get out there and strut your Deep Self in whatever way feels good for you at this moment on your journey of soul.

Strut is a tricky word. It certainly doesn't convey modesty. And it may suggest swagger and pomposity. But I mean it as shining your true, best Self outward, with fully unfurled self-love and self-assurance. You are most beautiful, powerful and nourishing to others when you show up confidently and completely as your Self. This is not about being better or more than another person. It is an inside-out strut that knows to honor yourself doesn't require you to diminish another. Quite the opposite is true. You encourage others to strut their best stuff as well.

When you strut your Deep Self, do so in an ethos of abundance. Individually and collectively, we are starving from a lack of soul-sourced authenticity. People are living their masks and roles, rather than their unique essence and gifts, and we all suffer as a result. So bring your best to the communal table of humanity, and encourage and embrace others who are choosing to strut their Deep Self and offer their best as well. Know that there is truly enough happiness, love, respect, worthiness and power to go around. The more we share from our gifts, in the spirit of giving generously and only taking what we need, the more abundance we create for everyone, and the more resources we can bring to bear on the economic, social and environmental issues that plague our world.

When we live in accordance with our best, life-centered instincts of goodness, grace and generosity, we are aligned with the ways of the Mother Earth, the sacred feminine and our inner Goddess Self. As Nature so gorgeously shows us at the Summer Solstice, and as you explored in the outer pathwork exercise, we are immersed in a waking dream of abundance where everything we need is being generously gifted to us, if we only have eyes to see and a heart to receive.

So strut your Deep Self and cast your goodness and best offerings out into our hungry world, and receive the goodness and offerings of others in kind. Trust that your blossoming matters, and that you can bring about positive change for yourself and others through your beauty and gifts. And in these ways, an ethos of abundance can take root and bloom in your life, family, workplace, community and our shared society, with each of us finding our true place and purpose within the great, glorious weaving of life.

LAMMAS

Harvest your life story:
seek out endings
and the seeds of the new.
One cycle ends
so another can begin,
in the waning light
of Lammas.

Lammas marks the end of the current cycle of your journey of soul. The Wheel of the Year has turned from darkness and death, through light and life, and now shines out the last of this season's light before a new cycle begins. So too you've come to the end of one turning of your journey; it's time to harvest its bounty of life lessons and personal growth, and to seek out the seeds of your next cycle.

At Lammas, the summer sunshine has baked the land a golden yellow. Fruits, berries and grains bend branches and stalks with their plump ripeness, ready to offer up their bounty to the harvest. Yet the outer look of things can be deceiving. Day by day, the light wanes and the dark waxes; cold will soon replace heat, and the powers of death overtake those of life. The balance has shifted, and the abundance that is now so evident will soon be gone.

Lammas is the pagan celebration of the early harvest, with grains, such as wheat and corn, playing a central role in the symbolism of this Sabbat. The golden fields of grain are ready for harvesting. What has been tended and brought to full fruition must now be cut down to feed hungry bellies. Some living things are sacrificed to nourish other living things, and to ensure the continuity and wellness of the whole. With death comes the miracle of rebirth, held within the seeds and their promise of a new harvest.

This theme of self-chosen, sacrificial death in support of life and rebirth infuses the mythic roots of Lammas. The Corn King, John Barleycorn and the Harvest King are some of the names given to the sacrificial God who gathers His energy into the crops that are cut down at Lammas to feed the living and to ensure a new harvest in Spring. In Celtic mythology, the Goddess Tailtiu cleared the land for cultivation as a gift to the people and died from Her tremendous efforts. Lammas is also called Lughnasadh, in reference to the Celtic God Lugh. Tailtiu is Lugh's foster mother, and legend has it that Lugh instituted a Lughnasadh harvest festival and games in Her honor.

Your journey of soul calls you to this same theme of self-chosen sacrifice in service of your personal healing and transformation. You must be willing to harvest your soul lessons and cut away those things that are now complete or that block your future growth. Some things must die in your life for something new to be born.

It is Lugh — the Shining One, the many-skilled God, bearing His Sword of Light — that illuminates your Lammas, harvest pathwork. Lugh meets you on a hilltop, offering you a wide viewscape that can help you see deep into the heart of your life story and the struggles of Mother Earth, as one cycle of your journey of soul and one turning of our humanity end, and a new cycle and turning begin. In these mysteries of life, death and rebirth, Lugh is your luminescent, loving guide as you embrace the incisive, demanding and often painful tasks that Lammas asks of you.

At its core, Lammas is a season of hope and the miracle of new beginnings. In the golden field that is your life story, you can find everything you need to heal your soul, transform your life and mend our world. Within you are the lessons, endings and seeds of powerful new beginnings that can lead you ever closer home to your Deep Self and authentic humanity.

A Sabbat Mystery
Lugh and the Miracle of a New Harvest

As the sun begins its downward arc toward the horizon, the God Lugh greets you on the summit of a hill, backlit by soft, descending rays of sunlight. His long, flaxen hair is tied back with a leather strip and He is dressed in the simple, handspun garments of the country folk who worked the land in ages past. He smells of sunshine, soil and sweet growing things.

In the circle of Lugh's shining presence, you feel safe, protected and nurtured. Somehow you know that everything He has to offer, He would gladly give to you and to others, and that wherever His blessed light touches the Earth, a natural abundance arises and flourishes.

With wide-sweeping arms, Lugh draws your attention to the panorama of golden fields that spreads out before you; tall, slender stalks of wheat bend and rustle in a hot wind, top-heavy and ripe for the harvest.

"Below us is the great exchange of life," He says, "the miracle of sunlight transformed into sustenance to feed the children of this hungry world. But there is a price to this miracle: what has come to full fruit must give its life to fill the bellies of the living; death is the price some things must pay to ensure the wellness and renewal of the whole."

A sword appears in His hands, its hilt toward you and the tip pressed against His breast.

"Everything has its season," He says, His blue eyes locking onto yours, "The seed of the new resides within the body of the living; the grain must be cut down for the seed to find fresh soil. All things of the material world are governed by this ever-repeating pattern; one cycle must end so another can begin."

Lugh gently moves His fingertips across your field of vision, and your consciousness shifts so you can view the landscape through His unclouded awareness. You take in the weaving of life that underlies the golden fields: the parched, barren soil, the particles of contaminants in the air, and the murky sludge in the nearby stream.

"Like the green-growing world, humanity has also come to the end of a cycle," Lugh says, "For millennia, your species has lost sight of the natural ways and rhythms of the Mother Earth. You have taken more than She can bear, and despoiled the air, water and land that sustain you. Now you are reaping what you have sown; this imbalance has come to a breaking point, threatening the very elements that support human life."

For a few moments Lugh is silent and you can sense the Mother Earth as He does, weighed down and weary, with Her living systems stressed and failing. And you know in your deepest heart that She is fragile and precious, and that Her stability and health are being severely jeopardized by our collective disrespect and maltreatment.

"I do not share these things to burden you with a vision of gloom and despair," Lugh continues, "Within everything are the seeds of a new season and a new harvest, and their miracle of a life-affirming new beginning."

The sword now appears with its hilt in Lugh's hand and its sharpened point pressing against your tender skin.

"You too have come to the end of a cycle on your journey of soul," Lugh says, "and your own healing and evolution are intimately intertwined with that of humanity and the Earth.

"The outer imbalance in the natural world and the malaise of humankind reside within you, side by side with your inner imbalance and discontent; each reflects and informs the other. And the seeds of the new are there as well, within your living body and life story. With these seeds, you can mend and renew your life and this world. But there is a price to be paid for this miracle; you must be willing to change in life-serving ways.

"You must ask yourself: what is ready to be harvested and cut away in my life in service of my soul work, and a more sustainable, balanced exchange between myself and the Mother

Earth? What lessons must I ingest to aid my transformation? What am I willing to sacrifice for new seeds to take root in my existence and the greater world?"

The sun now brushes the horizon and you feel the chill of the impending darkness. Lugh's light is dimming and you reach out to touch Him, and infuse yourself with His illuminating wisdom, wide-scope vision and truth-seeing powers.

A great sadness and sweet hope fill your heart, a knowing that a time of reckoning has indeed arrived and that you must change, humanity must change, if we are to preserve the beauty and abundance of the Mother Earth. Some things must end, must die, for something new to be born.

Lugh speaks to you one last time, "Remember that the seeds of the new are held within the body of the living. Everything you need to heal, grow and transform yourself and your world is present right now, in the golden field that is your life story. Be guided by your journey of soul, and the endings and new beginnings that naturally arise within you, moment by moment, and season by season. Be bold, be brave, be wise. From the depth of this cycle, a wondrous new beginning emerges."

With a sudden gust of wind, Lugh and the hilltop vision are gone, transformed into a descending spiral of golden chaff. And in your cupped hands are the seeds, the miracle, of the new harvest to come.

A Sabbat Teaching
The Seasons and Cycles of Breath

Our journey of soul is like breath.

On the in-breath, we enter deep inside ourselves, to the

wellspring of our soul and the mysteries of the sacred dark, seeking guidance and inspiration for our pathwork of healing and transformation, and the seeds of our beauty and wounding that are ready to return to the light of our waking consciousness.

On our out-breath, we turn our focus outward, embracing the enervating powers of light and life, and letting the seeds of our pathwork express and reveal themselves in the machinations of our everyday existence. Life is our teacher, bringing us the insights, energies and experiences we need to heal, grow and blossom in the sunlit world.

On our return in-breath, we gather up and take back inside everything that we have learned and experienced. We harvest our healing work and life story, and ingest their transformative lessons, letting them nourish and change us. And in this process, we become a newer, brighter and more present expression of our Deep Self.

The turning of the seasons is like breath.

On the in-breath, the natural realm turns inward as the balance shifts from light and life to darkness and death. Nature sinks into stillness and repose, while the land rejuvenates and the seeds of the new gestate in the belly of the dark.

On the out-breath, the returning light and warmth awaken the sleeping seeds of life within the land. Roots dig deep and green tendrils reach upward to bask in the sun. Everywhere in Nature, creation expands outward in a rampant, stunning display of the beauty and abundance of new and blossoming life.

On the return in-breath, the living Earth offers up the fruits of its labors for the harvest. The death and sacrifice of some threads of life ensure the nurturance and continuance of others. Yet nothing is truly lost, for contained within death are the seeds of a new season and a future harvest.

And then the cycle begins anew, always turning, never ending, one breath, one season, one chapter on our journey of soul is followed by the next. In these ways, life sustains and creates more life, and the light of our soul shines ever brighter.

Our busy modern world is not like breath. If anything, we are fixated on a perpetual out-breath, with its expansive, external focus. We are always doing and striving, charting our passage through life by the material markers of achievements and possessions. More is better. Growth is everything.

Yet we can never escape the natural order of things. We can't breathe out, without breathing in. The outer arises from the inner, and that which grows and expands, in the end, returns to the still, fertile center of things to feed and give rise to the next cycle of life.

Individually and collectively, we have reached the end of our extended out-breath. It is time to shift our focus to the return in-breath of harvesting and ingesting what we have learned from the fruits of our efforts, and of winnowing out what needs to die and be sacrificed in service of the balance and wellness of the whole. This is the work of Lammas, where profound, consciously chosen endings gift us with the seeds of profound, life-serving beginnings, and from these seeds our lives and our world are renewed and reborn.

Guided Meditation
The Golden Field of Your Life Story

On the day of Lammas, as the sun begins its descent to the horizon, find a place indoors or outdoors where you can feel the warmth of sunshine on your skin. Make yourself comfortable and ensure that the space and your time will be private and uninterrupted.

Close your eyes and begin to track the movement and energies of your breath. On your in-breath, sink deep, deep inside yourself and anchor within the core of your being. On your out-breath, feel your inner energies reach beyond your skin, mingling and communing with the outer world. On your return in-breath, draw these outer encounters back inside yourself, rich with the information and energies of your dance with otherness.

Continue to bring this quality of awareness to the movements and turnings of your breath, inner to outer and back to inner again. On your out-breaths, open yourself to the seasonal energies of Lammas, with Summer still hot upon the land, but with the powers of darkness waxing. On your return in-breath, draw in the smells of the sun-baked landscape, the changing quality of the light and however else late Summer manifests in your part of the world.

As you take these energies inside yourself, imagine them stirring up ancestral memories from our agrarian past, when Lammas was a crucial time of harvesting and storing grain for the lean winter months, and for the seeds of future harvests. Then go deeper still, opening yourself to the Lammas mysteries of death and sacrifice in service of life and rebirth.

When you feel filled up with these powerful Lammas energies, let them paint for you a flat hilltop with an expansive view of the surrounding landscape. Imagine a sunset-hued sky, with the sun descending toward the horizon. Then sense Lugh appear at your side.

Turn to face Lugh; take in the color of His eyes and hair, the look of His face and form, and the feel of His warm, all-encompassing presence. Clasp Lugh's hands in yours; feel His strong grip and the powerful currents that course through His fingertips — His are skilled, knowing hands that wisely wield the sword that brings death to ensure the wellness and renewal of the whole. Commune with Lugh, sharing words of welcome and connection.

Ask Lugh to guide you in your Lammas tasks of harvesting your soul lessons that have come to full fruition, and of discerning those things that must be cut away in service of your wellbeing and that of our world.

Lugh directs your awareness to the viewscape before you. See an expanse of cultivated land ready for harvest. This is the golden field of your life story that can show you many things, from pieces of your story and soul work that span your entire lifetime or that have come to light in your recent pathwork. It can reveal the micro details of a single memory, or the wider vista of your place and purpose in the weaving of greater human society. This field resides within you and is reflected in the outer manifestations of your life. It is always present, a storehouse of information and remembrances, to help you make brave, wise choices on your journey of soul.

With a palm held flat against your mid-back, Lugh fills you with His wisdom and truth-seeing powers. A beautiful sword, shining and sharp-edged, appears in your hand. When you gaze down at the surrounding landscape, it is as if you can see into the very heart and necessity of things.

Speak out loud your desire to be shown your soul lessons that are ripe and ready for harvest at this moment, in alignment with your highest good. Open yourself to whatever the field shares with you, be it words, images, sensations, emotions, memories, insights or information. Breathe these things deep into your body, ingesting their healing, transformative lessons, and letting them nourish and change you.

With your sword, carefully, lovingly cut away the old pieces of your life story and patterns that must now die away. Offer up this sacred chaff to the Mother Earth, knowing that She will honor your sacrifices and endings by transforming what you have cut away, in Her great composting belly, in service of new life.

Tenderly gather up the seeds of new beginnings and possibilities that reveal themselves in your winnowing work. For now, let the seeds be and do not probe any further into their contents. Hold them close to your heart, infusing them with your love and commit to follow where they lead in the next cycle of your journey of soul.

Take as long as you need for these essential Lammas tasks.

Feel Lugh behind you, with His hand still on your mid-back, filling you with His brilliance and love, and guiding your truth-seeing and cutting-away process with His broader awareness of the needs of all living things and of the Earth.

Through His touch, your awareness widens and you take in the whole of Mother Earth. You are a part of Her, and She is a part of you. Let yourself fully feel the power and importance of this primal connection: the Earth's breath is your breath; Her body is your body; Her wellbeing and stability are inseparable from yours; and your healing and transformation are Hers.

As your Lammas work comes to a close, visualize the last rays of sunlight melding with the contours of the landscape before you. With every passing day, the power of the sun fades and diminishes, and the seasons of darkness and death fast approach.

A parting is upon you and it is time to say goodbye to Lugh. Gaze upon His beautiful face, His love radiant still in the encroaching darkness. Share with Him your gratitude for His guidance and wisdom, and wish Him farewell.

The sun dips below the horizon and Lugh is gone, taking His sword with Him. Yet your hands are not empty. In their cupped interior are shining seeds that hold the dormant magic of your pathwork to come. Press your palms against your solar plexus, and take these seeds into the depths of your inner darkness, trusting that they will offer up their healing, transformative energies when the time is ripe.

Let your hilltop vision fade away, and use your breath to bring you back into your physical body and waking reality. When you open your eyes, take in the quality of the light as darkness begins to descend around you. As you finish your meditation, take a few minutes to check in with your emotions. Lammas can be a time of loss and sadness, and it also brings joy and hope. From endings and death, new life emerges. So the world and your life are forever renewed in the waning light of Lammas.

Inner Pathwork
To Harvest Your Life Story

In the midst of my journey of soul, when I was traveling through the darkest, most painful part of my personal story, a well-meaning friend told me to let go of my story, that the past was the past and it was time to move on. To this I replied, "I'll be done with my story when my story is done with me."

Our life stories are not blockages or burdens we must repress, cut away or transcend; they are the very lifeblood, our teachers and guides, on our journey of soul. We are meant to harvest and ingest the core lessons held within our stories, and only then will our stories be done with us.

Story, in this context, is the sum of our life experiences, including what has happened to us, our emotional and behavioral responses, and the meaning that we have layered onto these experiences and absorbed from our family and surrounding environment. Powerful experiences, both positive and negative, form the bedrock of our life story and have a tremendous influence on our self-concept and outer engagement of the world. The golden field image of the Lammas meditation is a metaphor for your life story.

Lammas is a reflective time of considering which parts of your story are ripe and ready for harvesting. The intention of this inner pathwork exercise is to explore and develop the skill of harvesting your story. To harvest your story is to allow yourself to remember, feel, experience and be changed by its contents. Set the intention to do this pathwork exercise in alignment with your highest good, and to only go as deep as is right for you at this time. Make sure you have the resources you need, including the help of a healer or therapist, if you find yourself in painful, disturbing remembrances.

Continue the deep introspective work you began in your Lammas meditation of harvesting and ingesting your soul lessons. Connect again with Lugh's truth-seeing powers and the images, memories and information that came to you in your Lammas vision. Delve further into this vision, with a more directed focus on your pathwork in the past twelve months, using the following questions.

What positive and negative events have happened in the past twelve months? What have you been dreaming about? Yearning for? Resisting? Wanting to change? What has been the focus of your pathwork in this time period? What seeds of beauty and wounding have you discovered in your Sabbat meditations and exercises, and in your other spiritual and healing practices? How have you worked with these seeds? How have they manifested in your life? What insights and experiences have come to you? What personal wounding, memories and issues have been triggered by your pathwork? What have you learned about your deeper beauty and sacred purpose? What new, beautiful transformations have you embraced? What else has shifted and changed for you? What feels complete and ready for harvest? What still feels stuck and needing attention? What needs to be cut away and sacrificed in service of your healing and wellbeing?

Allow these questions to stir things up in your inner landscape, and see what bubbles to the surface from the golden field that is your life story. Look for a common, recurring story, theme or pattern of responses that has a strong charge for you. Trust your intuition and emotions. Where there is energy and reaction, either positive or negative, you know you have found a story ripe for harvest.

Let your answers brew for awhile. Sleep on it and see what dreams come to you. Be open to flashes of insight or new information. Again, trust your intuition and emotions to see what part of your story wants your attention and has gifts to offer you at this time.

Once you have a sense of which part of your story is ripe for harvesting, you can further explore its content and energies through any kind of creative expression such as journaling, poetry, painting, sketching or dance. Imagine taking the story inside of you, ingesting its hidden meanings, lessons and gifts, and letting it speak to you through your creative process. Avoid indulging in analysis and problem solving; let this be a deep communion between you and your story, and let the story itself reveal its nourishing, healing, transformative offerings.

This Lammas exercise can be the start of a longer period of pathwork or therapeutic process of entering and harvesting your story's depth in search of its gifts of healing, change and seeds of the next cycle of your journey of soul.

Know that your life stories, be they joyful or painful, inspiring or despairing, hold the promise of a happy ending because their ultimate purpose is to lead you home to your beautiful, powerful Deep Self and authentic humanity. The stories themselves will guide you and return to you, as often and deep as is needed, for you to take in their transformative magic. You will know that you are done with a story when the story is done with you.

Outer Pathwork
Inner and Outer, Self and Other

An exploration with breath:

Find a private place outside or sit in front of an open window that looks out onto an appealing viewscape, preferably one with natural elements, like the open sky, trees and birds. With eyes open, follow the inner and outer movements and energies of your breath: anchor deep inside yourself on your in-breath, connect with the outer world on your out-breath, and draw these outer, mingled energies back inside of you on your return in-breath, anchoring once more in your core.

Once you have settled into this breath pattern, add another element to your focus. Notice what in the outside world is most strongly capturing your attention. It doesn't matter what it is, or whether it is from the human or natural realm, just go with whatever is calling to you. Open yourself up to this communion between your inner energy and this outer presence. On your out-breaths, feel this encounter touch and inform you. On your return in-breaths, sense the different quality of the energy you draw back into yourself, with a bit of you and a bit of this otherness. Continue this energetic communion for several breaths, absorbing it into your being, and letting it shift and change your inner landscape.

An exploration with emotion:

For the duration of one day, bring the same inner-outer, focused awareness that you used in your breath exploration to your emotional state and that of the people around you.

For part of the day, let your emotions follow their regular course, with your moments of joy, gratitude, curiosity, amusement, love, sadness, irritation, anger, fear, guilt or whatever emotional states naturally arise in you. If you have habitual patterns of emotional reactions, go with your normal flow, with no judgments, no blocking and also no over-indulging. Just be honestly who you are in your everyday interactions.

As your emotions rise up, witness each in turn. Notice how the emotion affects your outer expression: what you say and how you act. Pay close attention to the impact of your emotion on individuals around you: how they respond in words, actions and energy. And then feel the whole encounter, with the energies of your outer expression and others' responses, return to you. Heed how these mingled energies feel inside of you, and how they amplify or shift your emotions and responses.

For the rest of the day, reverse this exercise by focusing first on other people's emotions, as expressed in their words, actions and energies. Pay close attention to how you take their emotions and energies inside of you, and how this in turn affects your energetic and emotional responses.

An exploration with action:

For the duration of one day, indulge in planned and spontaneous positive actions, for people you know and for strangers.

For example, give your seat to someone standing on the bus, buy a coffee for the person in line behind you, bring cookies to the office, treat your best friend to lunch, call your parents and tell them you love them, buy a surprise gift for a child, or take your partner on a special outing. Load the day up with as many positive actions as possible.

As with your breath and emotion explorations, pay close attention to your inner state, as well as the outer responses of the recipients of your good deeds, and track the return of your shared energy and communion to your inner state. Really take in the goodness of your actions, and the goodness of others' reactions, and the quality and impact of these mingled energies on your inner landscape. How does each of your positive actions change you and your outer environment?

Lammas is a time of assessing your travels on your journey of soul in the past year, and of asking critical, probing questions to align yourself to your next cycle of healing and growth. Though the focus of this assessment is primarily on your individual pathwork, whatever you choose ultimately affects those close to you and the greater world.

The intention of these exploration exercises is to give you simple, direct experiences of this powerful truth: there is no separation between inner and outer, and self and other. Though we have physical boundaries woven of flesh, and psychological barriers woven of belief and action, still we are in constant, intimate contact with each other and our environment, sharing breath, sharing emotions, sharing actions and reactions, and beneath it all, sharing energy.

Bear this in mind as you assess your pathwork progress, harvest your soul lessons and decide what sacrifices and changes you need to make to continue to heal and grow in the cycle to come. Remember what it feels like to share your breath, emotions and positive actions with others. Consider the impact you have on those in your immediate environment, and the broader needs of our struggling humanity and fragile planet home.

Together with our fellow humans and the plants, creatures and powers of the Mother Earth, we are co-informing and co-creating this world. So give your very best to this sacred task, and let your every breath, emotion and action be a positive contribution to the wholeness that serves and sustains us all.

Walk the Path
The Miracle of New Beginnings

Lammas pathwork is analogous to the return in-breath on your journey of soul — of gathering up and taking back inside your last twelve months of pathwork — a pause moment of keen awareness, critical assessment and conscious engagement of what you have learned, what needs to be cut away, and what is coming next.

In the weeks to come, and as one cycle of your journey of soul ends and another begins, continue the deep, introspective work of your Lammas meditation with Lugh and inner pathwork of discovering, harvesting and ingesting the parts of your life story and soul lessons that have come to fruition.

Endings are natural outcomes of this work, as are new beginnings. To harvest wheat, you cut down the stalks and winnow the grains from the chaff; some grains become foodstuff and others become the seeds of the new har-

vest. Your personal pathwork is no different.

When a part of your life story is ready for harvest, you draw upon the sharp edge of your truth-seeing discernment to cut away your old ways of knowing, and separate out the grains of your soul lessons. In amongst these grains, you will find the lessons that are ripe in the present moment, and the seeds of lessons still to come. To ingest the ripe soul lessons is to take them inside of you and let them transform you. When you become something new, the old dies away, in part by the natural process of atrophy, and in part by your conscious choice to do things differently in the future and to end that which does not serve your transformative pathwork.

These choices and actions carve the pathway of your next cycle and gift you with the miracle of new beginnings. With this miracle, your journey of soul is reset and renewed, taking you ever closer to a life in alignment with the beauty and power of your Deep Self and authentic humanity.

The miracle of new beginnings not only resets your personal pathwork, it can also reset the trajectory of our greater society. We are living a pivotal, turning moment in our history. The Earth can no longer withstand our human excesses and disregard for the web of life that sustains us, and we appear to be on a collision course with ecological disaster.

Yet no outcome is inevitable. Lammas teaches us that as grains hold the seeds of a new season and a future harvest, so our lives hold the seeds of a new, different future. Everything we need to heal, grow and transform ourselves and our world are present in this now moment of our life story. But, and this is an essential but, Lammas also tells us that the miracle of new beginnings requires sacrifice, that something must be cut away, must die, for something new and better to grow in its place.

Collective change is driven by the choices and actions of individuals. As you experienced in the outer pathwork explorations, there is no separation between inner and outer, and self and other; we are co-informing and co-creating our world. Each of us must play our part if we are to turn the tides of our destructive ways and sow the seeds of a more sustainable, life-serving exchange between ourselves and the living Earth.

Include this wider, crucial awareness in your Lammas pathwork. As you heal old hurts and shed old patterns that do not serve your life, you mend the wounds and imbalances that jeopardize the wellbeing of the greater world. As you grow in love, acceptance and respect for yourself and others, you help create an ethos of love and respect that embraces all life on this Earth.

You are a part of the Mother Earth, and She is a part of you. By taking full responsibility for your own life in your Lammas pathwork, and engaging the soul lessons that can grant you positive, life-centered new beginnings, you grant this same miracle to the whole that encompasses and sustains our human society and planet home.

THE NEXT CYCLE

You find your way home
to Nature, your Deep Self,
the sacred feminine
one breath, one step, one season,
one cycle at a time,
constantly, courageously
beginning your life anew.

As this cycle on your journey of soul across the seasons comes to an end, Nature is shifting once more from the elemental forces of light and life to darkness and death as the last vestiges of Summer slip into the early signs of Fall.

Take a moment to step outside your door. Open your senses wide; drink in the light, colors, textures, sounds and smells of the natural elements that surround you; let these sensual encounters seep into your skin, down through your flesh and bones, into the very core of your being.

You are home, here amidst the physical wonders and swirling energies of the natural realm, here on this green and blue jewel of Earth as it spins and cycles its way through the infinite Cosmos.

Close your eyes and place your hands on your belly; track your inhalation, letting it draw your awareness into the depths of your inner landscape. Empty your mind; relax your body; be with yourself, still, silent, at ease.

You are home, here amidst the physical wonders and swirling energies that are you, here rooted in the beauty and gifts of your Deep Self and authentic humanity, a unique-in-all-the-universe being, spinning and cycling your way through your one, wondrous life.

With a soft, unfocused gaze, once again take in the surrounding landscape. On your exhalation, share a bit of your Deep Self essence with the outer world; on your inhalation, draw in the energies of sun, earth, wind and wild, green-growing things, and sense them infuse and inform your inner world. Breathe in, breathe out, slow, sweet, steady.

You are home, here amidst the love and rightness of this communion, within and without, between your Deep Self and Nature, spinning and cycling together through the seasons of light and dark, life and death, and joy and sorrow.

In all of these things — your body and the body of the Earth — your Deep Self and the essence of every living being — the powers and mysteries that govern the cycles and seasons of Nature and your life — the shining love that infuses and connects life to life in the infinite dance of Creation — you are home in the love embrace of the sacred feminine.

These essential connections are always present; you are already home. Your journey of soul, at its core, is about remembering, reclaiming and living, ever more deeply and profoundly, this simple, powerful truth. This process is an unfolding journey that begins anew with every breath, every step, every season and every cycle, in the big and small miracles that mark your healing and personal growth, and that bring positive, life-affirming change to the greater world.

Breathe deep and feel your feet upon the ancient pathway of the sacred feminine. Look behind you and bear witness to your Sabbat travels through one cycle of the Wheel of the Year, across its seasons of darkness, death, light, life, joy and sorrow — engaging the soul lessons ripe for you at this time, renewing your primal relationship with Nature and the Gods and Goddesses, and acquiring the knowledge and skills that facilitate your spiritual pathwork. You have walked this ancient path in your own way, following where your Deep Self and life story have led you.

You are not the same person you were at the beginning of this journey; you have become someone new, and this new isn't an ideal, perfected state, but a deeper, more present and beautiful you.

No matter how significantly you have changed or how messy your life still feels, love and embrace yourself as you are right now, honor the hard, hard work you have done, both the struggles and positive changes, and savor this sweet moment and the goodness that is your life.

Take another deep breath and look ahead to the new cycle and journey of soul across the seasons opening before you. The Fall Equinox approaches, once more beckoning you to descend into its mysteries of the sacred dark in search of the next pieces of your pathwork on your journey. Once more Nature, the Gods and Goddesses and the sacred feminine will offer you their seasonal wisdom and gifts that are both eternal and fresh to the moment.

And once more, you will return to the core themes of your soul work and life story, and their reflections in your beauty and wounding pathwork. Though it may sometimes seem like you are treading over old, familiar ground, know that you follow a spiral path that will lead you ever deeper into the layers and complexities of your unfolding soul work.

With your feet firmly on this ancient pathway, feel the fierce love, within and without, that beckons you forward on your journey of soul. Remember the seeds of new beginnings that came to you at Lammas. Renew your commitment to follow where they lead, and to once again step beyond the outer edge of your known world to source the deepest roots of your emerging pathwork. Then, consciously, courageously, joyfully take that step out of one cycle and into the next, and begin your life anew.

ACKNOWLEDGMENTS

The Path of She Book of Sabbats is the love child of my many years of communing with the Gods and Goddesses in the turning of the seasons, and Path of She's focus on the transformative ways of the sacred feminine that call us to embrace the light and dark, and beauty and wounding of our journey of soul. My deepest, forever gratitude reaches out to these Mysteries that have guided the cycles and seasons of humanity throughout the ages.

Many of my travels into the primal mysteries of the Sabbats have been in the company of the most extraordinary of spiritual companions. I would like to offer my profound appreciation to: Robert Birch, Kisae Petersen, Seraphina Capranos, Raven, Amy Phillips, and my Salt Spring pagan community.

To my ever-fabulous Path Tribe of kindred spirits, and to my Path of She readers and subscribers: thank you so much for your wonderful support, feedback and enthusiasm. To Julie Clark, Suzanne Michell and Shelby Johnstone: I am grateful beyond words for your creative input and critical support of my Path of She work.

Lastly, and always first in my heart, I thank my partner Larry and my son Nathan who are my beloved companions in all the seasons of my life. This book, and so many others wondrous things, could not have been possible without you by my side.

About the Author

Karen Clark is the author of *Tale of the Lost Daughter, The Path of She Book of Sabbats: A Journey of Soul Across the Seasons*, and the *Path of She Guided Journey Series.* As a writer, teacher and waking woman, Karen's passion is to return the Goddess and our sacred feminine nature back to their rightful place in our everyday lives.

Her Path of She work translates Goddess mysteries to our modern search for meaning, healing, personal growth, and collective transformation.

About the Path of She

The Path of She invites you on a journey of transformation with the sacred feminine to reclaim the lost beauty and powers of your Deep Self and authentic humanity. Rooted in pagan teachings and practices, the Path of She translates the ancient mysteries of the Dark Goddess to our modern needs and sensibilities.

To learn more about Karen and the Path of She, visit: **pathofshe.com** where you can subscribe to receive posts by email or listen to Path of She podcasts

Follow Path of She on: **Facebook, Twitter, Itunes and Android**

Books in The Path of She Series

Guided Journey Series

Each season expresses different aspects of the elemental forces that shape life on Earth, written large in the physical displays of Nature, and the Goddess mysteries that illuminate our human experience and life story.

Align your journey of soul with these seasonal offerings of Nature and the Goddess through a seven-lesson guided journey with integrated wisdom teachings, pathwork exercises, journaling tasks and a guided meditation.

Fall Journey

Your Hera's Path: Seeking Your Spiritual Roots

Winter Journey

Your Rebirth Magic: Braving the Great Below

Spring Journey

Your Whole/Holy Powers: Embracing Your Life Story

Summer Journey

Thou Art Goddess: Claiming Your Inner Goddess

OTHER PATH OF BOOKS

Tale of the Lost Daughter

Sarah Ashby, a rising, young financial executive, is a lost daughter. Despite her worldly success, she longs for something more, essential, precious, that's missing from her life, connected to her feminine soul.

Journey with Sarah as she heeds the call of her longings and sets off on a spiritual adventure to a rugged island on the Canadian West Coast, and the pagan world of ritual, magic, and the ancient Goddess Hecate. Here Sarah discovers the lost tales of She that can return the life-giving ways of the sacred feminine to her life and our world.

Made in the USA
Monee, IL
06 June 2020